1st Grade Therapy for Adults

For further information contact:

The Wayne Smith Company, Inc.
1300 L Street, N.W., Suite 1050
Washington, DC 20005

Photo by Victor Stekoll
Graphics by Blue Sky Graphics, Inc.
Cover Design by Robin Noble
    Robin Noble Design Management (703)845-1108

Dedicated to My Readers:

**YOU ARE PERFECT
AND HAVE
BELIEF SYSTEMS
THAT SAY
YOU ARE
NOT**

**Please let this book be your Roseta stone of therapy
guiding you to a more conscious life.**

This book is a collection of my observations, ideas and interpretations of a philosophy formed and practiced by an apprentice human being.

"I Am What I Am And That's All That I Am." Popeye, 1932

Acknowledgements

Robin Noble	My best friend, who suggested I write this book.
Sally Walker	My right arm
Jean Roncal	My left arm

My sons:

Johnny	His *Magna Cum Laude* and Phi Beta Kappa achievements makes me a believer in heredity.
Billy	"Dad, I support you 100%"
Mike	Yeah, but what if?
Christina	My 100% conscious, perfect granddaughter. "Let's play Cinderella - I'm CINDERELLA."

And to all of the authors and seminar leaders who's shoulders I stood on to write this book.

TABLE OF CONTENTS

Foreword and Chapter One

EVERYTHING WE EXPERIENCE FORMS A BELIEF SYSTEM: WE ARE WHAT WE BELIEVE

All of us are weary. We live with a vague and empty, "Is that all there is?" feeling. We are uneasy knowing we are not living up to our potential and are at a loss to do something about it.

We realize we do things that make no sense but when we look around, everyone is doing it. To be approved and accepted we "go with the flow." We smoke, drink, and eat too much. We get into destructive relationships. We feel guilty, anxious, stressed out, full of contradictions, worries, anxieties, regrets, and double binds.

When we get what we want, it hurts even more because satisfying our wants isn't the answer either. At least when you don't get what you want, you can blame your misery on *that*.

There are too many unanswered questions.

Why is it possible to predict people's behavior in many situations? Why do people overreact in some situations and not in others? Why do people remain stubborn for hours over a small issue? Why are some people rich and happy and others rich and unhappy?

Where was I before I was born? Where are my roots? Why am I afraid to die? Where am I going after death and how do I get ready? And what am I suppose to be doing between birth and death? Will I live and die and not leave a mark?

Where is the delight? As children, we were all happy, joyful, healthy, optimistic. What happened?

There are many intelligent people who have figured out the answer to these questions. They have discovered how to live life productively with peace of mind, happiness, and vitality. Even though the books are full of knowledge and answers, they are written at such a high level, most people cannot follow them.

How do we create a bridge so that the information can cross over to all the people?

HOW CAN WE HELP PEOPLE TO HELP AND UNDERSTAND
THEMSELVES BY THEMSELVES?

If you can reduce complicated phenomena to a few simple rules, great leaps of understanding can occur.

Therefore, to simplify this book and to create a "bridge" so that this information can be communicated to all people, I will call a broad range of problems "belief systems."

This book is a simple explanation of a complicated subject that will help you understand enough to realize you can change your life, your past, your future, and your destiny.

If we were to study math, I would say we were at the level of 1+1=2. After we learn addition and subtraction, we will feel better and more confident about progressing further. Calling everything a belief system is very broad, but understandable enough to get you started so someday you can read the more complex, helpful, therapy books.

The essence is that we are programmed unconsciously by random and calculated observed events in our lives from which we create belief systems that automatically determine our behavior. As a result, we do not operate out of our own free will.

We lose vitality and become miserable.

The problem is that each person on this earth is different. Every second of each of our lives was perceived differently by each one of us. Only <u>you</u> know exactly what <u>you</u> are and how <u>you</u> got that way. And <u>I</u> only know exactly what <u>I</u> am and how <u>I</u> got that way. Only <u>you</u> can help <u>you</u> and only <u>I</u> can help me. We have to search ourselves to know ourselves.

Many people are unaware that being full of anger, worry, anxiety, or depression is an emotional disease that can be cured. The worse off you are, the less you know it. People who are unhappy, sad, or ill have been that way for so long they cannot remember anything else. Besides, therapy is expensive. And, what would people say if they found out you were going to a shrink?

You are an outside representation of your inner belief systems. Therefore, if you can change your inner belief systems, you can change <u>who you are</u> and eliminate what triggers you to suffer. You were not born with any of these belief systems. Getting rid of belief systems is a second chance to "go for it."

The way to neutralize our belief systems is to recall the random event that created the original belief system and reexperience it (i.e. relive it emotionally and physically) the same way it originally happened.

You Can Change the World!

Everybody wants to change the world for the better but feel powerless to do so. Now you don't have to be. Change yourself and you will change this world and the future generations that follow you.

Researchers tell us that Revolutionary, Religious, and Nationalistic changes are ignited by promises of spectacular better opportunities in the conditions of life. <u>This book promises an inner</u>

spectacular change of the personality for the better.

We are all battle weary veterans of the internal struggle to control our emotions and bad habits, and nothing will excite us more than victory over our hated lifetime internal foes. I speak of anxiety, worry, depressions, jealousy, smoking, overeating, and so forth.

THE ELIMINATION OF ANY ONE OF THESE WILL CHANGE A PERSON'S LIFE; AND I PROMISE THAT THIS BOOK HAS THE POTENTIAL TO CHANGE AND ELIMINATE ALL OF THEM.

This book describes how to discover and remove a belief system the same way you show someone how to mop a floor. Once you have learned how to mop a floor, you are able to mop any floor without supervision. The same is true regarding removing belief systems.

All you have to realize is that you are programmed and eliminate what creates your problems. After that the real you will emerge. You do not have to believe anything new! You can change your life dramatically in a few hours. You can show other people how to do it. What you know can be transmitted to all.

Did you ever wake up in the middle of the night and stumble around helpless in the dark because you could not see? Then you turn on the lights and all you need to know for the moment is there. You feel in charge and powerful. This is the feeling that comes over you when you eliminate a belief system.

Eliminating a belief system is like popping the cork on a bottle of champagne. Tremendous energy is set free. The more you eliminate belief systems, the better it gets.

Once you realize how a belief system controls you and that you can eliminate worry, resentment, insecurity, depression, loneliness, hate, revenge, and jealousy, you become light in spirit, more conscious, and tolerant of others, it becomes a joy just to be alive!

It is said that: "On the way to Heaven is Heaven!" The journey is all that there is! However, you do have to make a conscious decision to begin! In reality, there is no end. The moment your journey begins, you are in heaven! There is no place to get to. There is only the way or the path and your position on the path.

Some of us are fortunate to be on a spiritual path.

Billions of people do not know a path exists! By eliminating belief systems, each generation will pass less on to the next. In this way, the world will be transformed from the bottom up.

The book's intentions are:

1.   To help the reader to discover and eliminate their unconscious belief systems creating self-esteem, vitality and "The Desire To Know". The information is already available in books, films, and other learning experiences. The problem is to get people to be able to understand it.

        If enough people read this book and share it with their families, relatives, and friends, they will all experience the joy, relief, and feelings of expansion that come from eliminating a belief system. They will experience consciousness with each other.

        Their experience will contribute to a collective background of knowledge concerning consciousness and eliminating belief systems.

2.   My long-term goal is to create a multi-language world center where teachers can come to remove individual belief systems and learn how to assist children with same upon their return; to create computer programs and video tapes, so

that adults and children can remove belief systems in the privacy of their homes.

Can you imagine a world where everyone is removing belief systems on a daily basis? If belief systems separate us, what a "coming together party" there will be. The world could change for the better as fast as the Berlin Wall came down.

3.   Contribute to peace by presenting steps for eliminating The "War" belief system.

However, this is more than a self-improvement book. My hope is that the people who benefit from this book will be attracted together to take action. Our future depends on people coming together to accomplish global transformation.

                              NOTE

If any statement in this book upsets you, look upon it as an opportunity to discover a belief system.

Please don't get upset with the book. If the book called you a yellow-monkey, you would not get upset. Why? Because you are not a yellow monkey.

If you do get upset, look not on the page, but inside you for the inserted belief system that is triggering your upset. Treat the upset as an opportunity. (See Chapter 12: Crisis As An Opportunity.)

Chapter Two

BELIEF SYSTEMS

"'I believe' is a death chant!
'I believe' is a lock on free will,
a killer of the heart, a murderer of your feelings!"

Belief systems are self-inserted conscious and unconscious combinations of passed on information from all the senses (feel, touch, taste, see, and hear, etc.) They include the accepted agreed upon wisdom of a particular time in a specific location, "hear-say," dogma, rumor, tradition, bedtime stories, the Bible; indeed, a wide range of sources.

You can have belief systems about emotions like happiness, boredom, anger, grief, fear, or about senses, or any combination of the above. Besides coming from real experiences, belief systems can be formed from imagination, dreams, and fantasies. Whatever the perception, it becomes a part of a belief system.

These belief systems create unconscious automatic behavior. In other words, we are <u>not</u> aware when we do something, versus being aware or conscious.

(The unconsciousness I refer to in this book is the condition of the mind when it is not in the present. Have you ever driven a car ten miles and cannot remember it? Have you ever left your house and could not remember if you locked the door? Where was your mind at these times? It was unconscious or not present. To operate out of a belief system, your mind has to be unconscious.

All belief systems are bad because you are unconscious of them,. When you are conscious of a belief system and consciously choose to let it remain, it is alright because the belief system no longer has the power to control you in an unconscious manner.)

The emotional and physical input of the original event form the content of the initial belief system. Thereafter, each time a similar physical or emotional action occurs, in present day time, it triggers the initial belief system and the original reaction.

Each original event creates one or more belief systems which create automatic responses to future similar circumstances. **As a result, we are unable to judge or react to a present experience, because a previous belief system about the initial experience controls our ability to respond spontaneously.**

For example, do you remember the last lemon you bit into? Close your eyes, relax, calm down, take a few slow deep breaths, and see yourself biting into a lemon, the juice squirting into your mouth.

What body feelings are you having? What happens to your mouth? What other past memories of lemons can you recall? What is your first memory of a lemon? Your belief systems about lemons are connected to your original memory of lemons.

The first lemon you experienced in life created a belief system about lemons. Your second experience with lemons, was combined with the first, to create a combined belief system about lemons. Each subsequent lemon incident has either an identical or similar emotional or physical response as to the original. Your response to biting into a lemon will always be the same as the original belief system formed the first time you ate a lemon.

Just now, your mouth was on automatic and your feelings were unconscious. In fact, you did **not** just eat a lemon but your body reacted to the triggered belief system already inserted in you, as if you had just eaten a lemon.

What we believe forms us. Everything happens from inside out. A sexual thought precedes a sexual response. At any given instant, we are the sum total in material form of what we believe inside. What we believe will happen, will happen. The brain attempts to make sense out of every belief system, real, imagined, whether passed on over eons of time, or yesterday's observations. Your belief systems form your personality (ego).

Everything we know and experience is created by either individual or collective belief systems. We experience it, create a belief system about it; and then we perceive it that way forever automatically, unless we consciously examine it.

We are a product of our accumulated belief systems not our accumulated knowledge. We are products of what we believe not of what we know; and our major beliefs are formed in our earliest years before memory, before we could even read.

Compared to all the time we have lived, we have few memories. Where is the rest of our lives? Why don't we remember it? We remain unconscious of much of our behavior because most of our belief systems were inserted before memory.

How conscious you are determines how alive you are. The more belief systems you have, the less alive you are. Imagine consciousness as a pie. A belief system reduces the pie to a tiny piece. As the belief system grows, it narrows the tiny piece to a sliver. Instead of being the whole pie, the person loses himself in the sliver and forgets he ever was the whole pie. Narrowing and limiting consciousness is a form of death.

An elevator is a great example of how belief systems work. You are the elevator and the buttons are the belief systems. Trigger button #3 and you always get the third floor. The elevator and you do not have a choice. You can only go up or down--not sideways or diagonally. Mostly, other people or circumstances trigger your buttons. You just react unconsciously.

Imagine a computer delivered to your house with a written program in it of which you are not aware, and you have your **own** operating system. We are the way we are because of belief systems inserted in us before and after we were born. Before we had awareness. Before we had memory.

We don't know who we are, how we got this way, or why we do things the way we do. We don't know where we came from, what we are doing here, or where we will be going after death, but we have a lot of belief systems about such topics.

How we relate to people, situations, even objects, are belief systems. Every war, calamity, murder and rape, are the results of belief systems. When you see a person smoke, eat too much sugar, twitch, bitch, or create stress, misery, or excitement, it's a belief system in action.

Belief systems give us second hand life. Belief systems trigger automatic robotic behavior; the past over and over again. Stale bread, never fresh! In all cases belief systems are <u>not</u> real.

A belief system is a fact-proof-screen against reality. Reason and present day senses are not allowed to penetrate. The belief system insulates the self from the world as it really is.

<u>Not</u> the past events themselves, but our belief systems about past events control us. That we do not know the future is not a problem. That we have a belief system that says we should be upset if we don't know the future is a problem and it makes us miserable.

The ability to eliminate a belief system is literally the power to create a new personality and future for ourselves.

If you were not born with it, its a belief system. You can imagine anything and accomplish it if you do <u>not</u> have a blocking belief system. Most people board an airplane effortlessly. Others cannot even visit an airport. Eliminate belief systems about airplanes and you can fly!

A belief system will form to conceal something. For instance: Bravado will hide insecurity. How many people do you know that act tough, when they are really scared?

Ten people can experience the same movies and each come away with a different set of belief systems. Another belief system can block each person from ever being conscious about it again throughout a lifetime.

If you have a belief system that says, "You have to impress people with what you know," then you cannot tell your teacher what you do not know. This one belief system can stop all learning.

Being able to say I don't know would create less confusion. If we have a belief system that says we have to know, then we will make up answers. This is especially dangerous to vulnerable children, who truly trust us.

Are your beliefs good for you or harming you? Take a look at yourself: Are you in good or bad health? Do you do meaningful work? Are you happy or sad, rich or poor? Is evil going on around you? Your belief systems created these conditions.

Why would anyone that could see the stars, feel the sun and the warm breeze, smell the flowers, and hear the ocean, be convinced each workday to drive one hour in traffic, sit in an enclosed area for eight hours doing uninspiring work in a sweaty city? Your belief systems say you must do that.

If you have a belief system, "I must survive," you cannot just enjoy yourself or do the best job possible. You do what you have to do because you have a belief system that says you won't survive if you don't. Instead of enjoying yourself each day by doing a good job for the joy of it, you do it to survive.

No belief system will form when a person is doing exactly what they want to be doing. We are happy in the now, the present moment. You don't need anything when you are busy doing what delights you. You need love, a wife, a drink, or a hug when you <u>stop</u>. It's the pause that needs the belief system and it is not refreshing.

Why is it easy to remember the words of a song and so hard to remember the words of a poem? Different belief systems: possibly because poems were homework and songs were connected with parties and fun.

Why is it that music can be shared by all kinds of people in all countries over centuries of time? It can't be a belief system. It is a oneness. It is common to all.

When you realize people are operating out of belief systems, you take things less personally. Even the most bizarre behavior that might have frightened you in the past, now becomes only a passing curiosity. Just another belief system. Ho! Hum! Life becomes very interesting and you become more tolerant.

Gravity is <u>not</u> a belief system. Gravity knows what it is today and will be tomorrow. It is always there. It is not a substitute for something else. It is consistent and complete and does not change. We are all one with gravity, but our belief systems number in the trillions. Gravity works. Belief systems do not.

Without belief systems, human beings would be pure consciousness and have consistent and positive characteristics like gravity. Can you imagine what would happen if gravity did not have integrity, did not keep it's word, or decided not to show up for even one minute?

Belief system accumulation is accelerating. It is so rampant that it literally covers the earth. Television creates belief systems in millions of people every hour of every day. We absorb messages unconsciously. In fact, all we are is our belief systems. Whenever we talk or argue or communicate, we cannot help but infect each other with our belief systems.

The world today is slowly becoming uninhabitable. We have violence, poverty, war, lots of sorrows. People cause these problems. These problems represent and reflect our belief systems. The violence in the world is the total sum of our individual belief systems about violence.

What does it mean "to be"? If you are covered by belief systems, do you exist? If you are never anything but your belief systems, then your belief systems exist, but do you?

If we could be born and not inherit passed down belief systems formed centuries ago, our minds would be free to realize that without belief system, all is God--you, me, the fish, the birds, everything.

IT IS AS USEFUL AND BENEFICIAL TO DISCOVER AND ELIMINATE BELIEF SYSTEMS IN PEOPLE AS IT WOULD BE TO DISCOVER A CURE FOR CANCER. WITHOUT BELIEF SYSTEMS, THERE WOULD BE NO CANCER OR DISEASE.

My hope is that the final chapter of history will be written documenting how people on earth eliminated sufficient belief systems to enable them to take control of their destiny. Common planetary goals like peace and cooperation will then have a chance.

We will realize what we do affects each other.

Belief System Puzzle

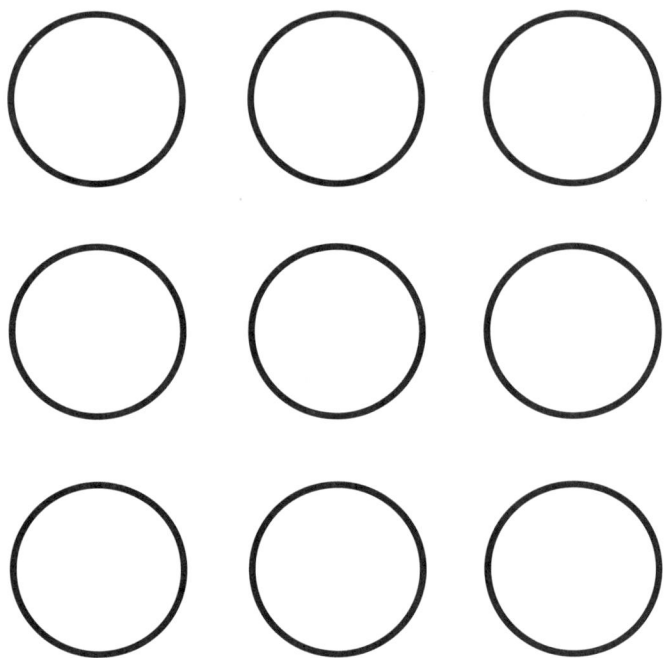

Can you cross all nine dots in
the above drawing with only four
straight lines without lifting your
pencil from the paper.

See page ___58___

Chapter Three

BELIEF SYSTEMS INSERTIONS

Observation

There is the story of the five year old girl riding in the car with her father. While stopped at a red light, he asked her what the red light meant. She said, "stop." When asked about a green light, she said that meant "go." "And, how about yellow?" inquired the father. "That means hurry up," she said.

"Hurry up" is an example of a belief system inserted unconsciously through observation. No one knew of the insertion, or when it happened, including the child.

The child could also observe and unconsciously insert:

1. Do not assume power or authority.
2. Do not be responsible.
3. Avoid health. Smoke, drink, use salt and sugar.
4. Avoid self-discipline.
5. Blame other people.
6. Create a harmful relationship to avoid loneliness.
7. Do not grow up.
8. Be dependent and gain no self-confidence.
9. Do not think, but accept things.

We observe whatever we do or think. When you observe, you acquire information. Most of this observation is unconscious. As human beings, we are interested in knowing and doing whatever helps us to survive. We observe how other people survive and insert belief systems into ourselves in order to survive. If we observe our parents under constant strain and stress and surviving, then we will create a belief system that says: "In order to survive, I must have stress and strain in my life."

Whatever we observe creates a new belief system or reaffirms an old one. We continue throughout our life to insert unconsciously millions of belief systems by observation. The result is that we are unconscious about most of our behavior. We automatically and unconsciously pass on these belief systems to future generations.

Almost everything people tell us from the day we are born, someone originally told them. It is all dogma, hearsay and folk tales! These belief systems are thousands of years old. Do they still apply? What was a fact and believed by everyone five hundred years ago can easily be viewed now as only a belief system. "No one can fly." "The earth is flat." Back then, these belief systems were never questioned.

We all enter this hypnotic sleep unknowingly, a sleep from which we are never awake or gain awareness again. Throughout our lives, we always justify our observed belief systems without ever examining them objectively. Some of our belief systems probably trace their origins back to the ape man.

The younger a person is when a belief system is inserted, the more controlling and unconscious it will be. Some examples:

Suppose as a 3-year old child (before memory), you received a red apple from a man wearing a black suit. The apple made you happy. You could form a belief system from this incident that the colors black and red are very good. As a result, you would <u>automatically and unconsciously</u> wear black and red clothes when you wanted to feel good.

Suppose the apple had a worm in it. You might have

formed many belief systems such as:

1.   "The color black is not good."
2.   "The color red is not good."
3.   "Black and red are okay together, but not apart."
4.   "Apples have worms in them, don't eat them."
5.   "Men in black suits are bad."
6.   "Men who give apples to children are bad."
7.   All the above plus more.

Continuing with this example, later in life as an adult, you meet a man with a black suit who wants to give you an apple. Based on your previous belief systems, you may refuse to take it without knowing why. You may not want to have anything to do with people who wear black clothes. You may talk to your friends everyday, except when they wear black. You may not like apples, may never remember the worm, and thus never recognize why you don't like apples.

A failure in love or work causes us to seek support. Whatever occurs when we seek support will end up as a belief system.

If, as a little boy, I suffer failure and run to my mother for support and she hugs me and makes the world a better place and just happens to be wearing a white dress and Chanel Number 5 perfume, then, depending on what kind of an individual I am, the following possible belief systems could develop:

1.   If I want to be hugged, suffer failure.
2.   If you want the world to be a better place, hug your mother or maybe hug any woman.
3.   I may always feel the world is a better place whenever I see the color white.
4.   Women in white dresses will hug you.
5.   Women that wear Chanel Number 5 will hug you.
6   Women in white dresses that wear Chanel Number 5 will create failure.

Other Examples

A hymn is a great example of a deeply entrenched belief system. ("Oh Lord, I am not worthy that thou should come to me.") Says who? Every Sunday, during the most impressionable years of your life, hymns may have been tattooed onto your unconscious brain. Every thought, action, feeling that you had listening to the hymn is still there, and you will relive it whenever it is triggered. Play the song and you feel unworthy.

The average person is full of "hymns" about religion, sexual behavior, eating, working, fear, guilt, doubt, anxiety, self-esteem, charity, love, self-confidence, success, failure, death, birth, hate, and more. The average person doesn't know that he or she has these belief systems. If you saw it and realized it was there, you would not know what it was, or where it came from.

Music can be used to form Belief Systems.

Lullabies
>	create belief systems about calming down and falling asleep.

Love songs
>	create belief systems about true love, everlasting love, lost love, sex and love.

Military or Marching Songs
>	create belief systems about a hero's death, permission to kill, romanticized views of war.

Church music
>	creates belief systems about God.

Work music
>	creates belief systems about working together for a great cause.

Fairy Tales create deep belief systems. For instance, The Big Bad Wolf creates a belief system that wolves are bad, while Little Red Riding Hood is good. Santa is great--so is Casper the Friendly Ghost. However, most ghosts are scary. Serpents are devils in disguise.

Christmas belief systems cause incredible destructive body stress. A stress test on parents and relatives on the eve of Christmas would give a heart doctor a stroke!

Who has not felt the pressure to please on Christmas morning? Who has not experienced the fear of loss of love, of being alone, of not cooking the food well, of being disappointed or disappointing, the overload of work, the crushing burden of debt? Christmas beats us psychologically worse than a slave master.

Many people enjoy Christmas, but others are disappointed. We all have belief systems that say "Everybody is happy on Christmas," yet many are not because they hold belief systems that lead them to expect more than they actually receive. Thus, we feel disappointed at the close of the day.

Have you ever seen a Christmas story on TV that did not have a happy ending? Have you ever seen a Christmas story where the mother has a nervous breakdown and the father a heart attack trying to please everyone? Where people who are alone break out in hives or cry all day?

Retailers would not advertise on that channel. As children, we are not aware of the sacrifices and work of loved ones to make our little face light up the room with delight. Before we reach the age of reason, we have belief systems that tell us Christmas is absolutely perfect, wonderful, and fulfilling. We also have belief systems that say we must preserve this fantasy for our children at all costs or lose their love.

Reality reveals that Christmas is an unhappy time for a lot of people even painful. One thing for sure, it isn't perfect even for the kids. How come we know so little about the misery? Because we have belief systems that do not let reality in. We repeat this misery every year. We pay financially for it for months. The stress caused by emotional burnout shortens our lives.

New Year's Day belief systems say we should have a great time yet many end up with a hangover.

Each of us receives hundreds of messages like this while growing up. We still operate out of these childhood belief systems and teach them to our children. What belief systems are you helping to insert in your children?

1.   Don't Waste Food!
     People in China are starving. As a child, I wasn't about to dispute my mother. However, if I ate all my food, how did that help a starving kid in China? If I didn't eat the food, how did it help?

2.   During World War II, "Japs" and Germans were no good. Now Americans want their children to grow up and be productive workers like the Japanese.

3.   Wear clean underwear in case you are in a car accident. You don't want people to find out you don't wear clean underwear. Is there someone at the scene of an accident checking for dirty underwear?

4.   What will <u>they</u> think? Who are <u>they</u>? Where are <u>they</u> hiding? Where do <u>they</u> get the time to watch me? Who pays <u>them</u>? What are <u>they</u> trying to catch me doing? Who watches them? To whom do they squeal?

5.   Never mind, you wouldn't understand! I understood it all except for the part I was asking about.

6.   She is a fast girl and just wants to have a good time. So did I.

7.   Sex is bad. Imagine my horror when I found out my mother was doing it with my father.

8.   People who have a different religion are unfortunate or uninformed or both. They are not going to heaven.

9.   Certain races are inferior. Certain races are superior (ours), but don't brag about it. Just know it.

10.   If you are rich, you are bad and/or did something bad to get the money. Happiness is money. Success is money. Rich people are smarter than poor people. Money is scarce. There is never enough.

11.   Don't take a risk, you'll lose.

12.   Don't let anyone hear you crying. Keep a stiff upper lip. (How?)

13.   Don't tell anyone good news. They will think you're bragging or worse, ask for a loan!

14.   Don't holler in the house, the neighbors will hear you. I could hear the neighbors hollering, why shouldn't they hear me? We always listened when they hollered.

15.   Pick up your room. Stay neat. There weren't enough closets. I didn't know where everything went.

16.   Unions are "good" and/or "bad".

17.   Our side is always right in wars.

Unconscious Childhood Belief System Insertions

#1

A young child needs a mother's "mothering." If it isn't there for some reason, the child will create a substitute for that love and survive by forming a belief system that says: Whenever I feel the need for motherly love, I will create a substitute for it. The substitute could be an aunt or big sister, or it could be consuming food.

#2

A second child faced with a similar need will form a belief system that says: When I need motherly love, I will get depressed and withdraw. In both cases, a belief system that limits the personality of the child has been formed. Neither person has a choice when faced with the need to be mothered. One will automatically seek out an aunt, sister, or food, and the other has no choice but to withdraw.

#3

A baby girl in a dark room tries to climb out of her crib and ends up hurting herself. She forms a belief system that says, dark rooms will hurt you. The rest of the person's life is spent avoiding dark rooms without ever knowing why.

Her husband constantly complains about the electricity bill because she won't turn any light off in the house. Today, this woman could do a "process" and recall the original incident, and once discovered and eliminated, the control held by the belief system will disappear forever.

#4

When new babies cry, something good will soon happen for them. A hug, a warm breast full of food, a diaper change. All great feelings. A belief system forms: "When I cry, something good happens. Therefore, whenever I want something good to happen, I will cry."

This may explain why some people never stop crying. A whining eighty year old person could be operating out of a belief system formed soon after his or her birth eighty years ago.

The above belief system can be used to justify all manner of behavior. For instance, a person who has had success whining for things could, in an escalation of this belief system, create a real disease like cancer to prove her whining is worthy of gaining approval or pity.

Death from cancer would be a final confirmation of the validity of all her whining over eighty years, plus leaving the entire family guilty until their own death. Meanwhile, this whining person may never have been conscious of the game she played throughout her life.

#5

A mother walks into her daughter's house and complains the dishes are dirty and the floor isn't clean. The daughter breaks into tears. The mother doesn't understand why her daughter is crying. The daughter doesn't have a clue as to why she burst into tears. What has happened is that they have triggered each other's belief systems.

The mother carries a belief system that says, "I only get attention from my daughter when I complain." The daughter has one that says, "The only way I can get my mother to stop criticizing me is by crying." These buttons are at an unconscious level and will create the same reaction until death. How did it all start?

History

One time in the past, possibly for only an instant, the mother felt unloved or ignored by the child. The child loved the mother, but was busy being a child. Instead of asking the child, "Hey kid I don't feel loved by you right now - DO YOU LOVE ME?" The child likely would have said: "Yes mommy, I love you very much." They would have hugged and been happy ever after.

Instead, the mother complained and made the child feel unloved. The feeling of being unloved was very painful and the child started to cry. The crying caused the mother to stop complaining. She now had the child's attention, if not her love. The child, by crying, has discovered how to stop the mother from complaining.

Two people who loved each other formed belief systems at that moment that has been separating them ever since! Now, the mother gets attention but no love, and the child gets to cry when people complain. Neither the child nor the mother is conscious of their belief systems that will last forever.

The flowing love they had for each other is now restricted, replaced by belief systems creating behavior that makes both of them miserable.

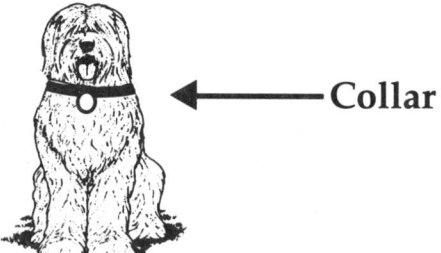

In-Ground Wire

Collar

Chapter 4

INFORMATION ABOUT BELIEF SYSTEMS

Training Dogs And People

Most people perceive life and people's intentions as very complex. <u>This is not so!</u> People operate and behave automatically and predictably from belief systems. People and dogs are trained and programmed the same way.

The procedure for training a dog involves <u>self-inserting</u> a fact or idea into their head which will create automatic behavior under certain circumstances. Pain or pleasure can be the facilitator. Once its been done, you can tether a two-ton dog with a shoe string and he won't attempt to break free. This is called forced conditioning and it creates a belief system that will control the animals behavior until death.

Let us say we want a dog to stay on the property. We wire the boundaries and put a collar on the dog that will shock the dog whenever he approaches the wire. Soon the dog will learn that if he stays on the property he will not get a shock. He will have developed a belief system about the property.

This belief system was self-inserted using pain as a facilitator and will stay with the dog permanently. Without consciously thinking about why, the dog never leaves the property. People or dogs operating out of belief systems <u>will always</u> respond to the same or similar situations with the same behavior.

Once you know a person's belief system, you can predict their behavior. You can upset them and calm them down. They have no choice. The only difference is that the dog's trainer has a plan and a goal for the dog. Humans just keep inserting belief systems without rhyme or reason. Your mind is no more free than a dog in a yard surrounded by fences. Belief systems are fences of the mind.

Flashes Of Consciousness

At present, all progress is being accomplished by flashes of consciousness that penetrate our belief systems temporarily. Over and over, we hear about people who had a gut feeling, idea, revelation, dream, insight, a feeling of joy, bliss, oneness, and connectedness to all things. These moments are flashes of consciousness that pierce the belief systems. We call it God, spirit, essence, psyche, inner being, grace, or soul.

It is consciousness eagerly waiting to serve us. It is you without belief systems. Who drives the car while you are day dreaming? Who wakes you up in the middle of the night to alert you to danger? When we sit still, we talk to ourselves. Who is this other person we are talking to? Each one of us has been in touch with something from within. Why do we ignore it? Suppose it is God. Suppose you are God!

Except for flashes of consciousness, belief systems automatically control our lives night and day. Once you have accumulated your major belief systems, your destiny is virtually set in concrete. Knowledge or facts that contradict a given belief system will be ignored. You will live out your life not living it at all.

Belief Systems Take Away God

We all feel there is an unfillable hole inside us. This hole was created at birth by replacing God with a belief system.

We are born in complete conscious communication with all in the universe (God); a delightful oneness, the only true merge we will ever know. Then, belief systems take over.

At birth while the infant is experiencing this delightful conscious communication with the universe, he or she experiences the pain of birth similar to the dog receiving a shock. The baby stops doing whatever it was doing and creates a belief system that says, "Whenever I am conscious and communicate with the universe, I suffer pain. Therefore, in order to survive and avoid pain, I must <u>not</u> communicate with the universe." We are less than a minute old and we have lost our ability to merge.

This belief system if <u>not</u> uncovered and eliminated, will last until death! Since few, if any of us, remember our moment of birth, what are the chances of filling in the hole?

This hole represents the delightful part of reality that is missing. Like a treasured doll or charm, we don't feel right without it. We search in vain and feel empty. We are lonesome for communication with God. Life is second hand, not real. We are born into the exact point we are forever seeking.

Cultural Belief Systems

Belief systems shared by a family, group, or nation are called cultural belief systems. The cultural belief system is continually inserted from birth on by <u>constant observation</u>. Consider, for example, food.

When humans are born, they can distinguish only four tastes: salt, sweet, sour, and bitter. People are born with a preference for sweet foods and a dislike for bitter ones. (In prehistoric times, this passed on knowledge was very useful. Wild sweet plants are generally nutritious. Bitter ones are often poisonous.)

If we were not born with a preference for certain foods, how is it explained that all over the world, people have food preferences? Mexican children like what is fed to them by their parents. The same for American, Chinese, and other nationalities.

All of us live from the belief system our culture gave us. We like hot dogs, while Mexicans like tacos. Once a belief system about food is inserted, you operate from it unconsciously and automatically.

When you are hungry, your ego will trigger your belief systems regarding food. A Mexican's belief system will require Mexican food, like salsa or a tamale. An American's hunger will filter through their belief systems and crave a hot dog.

The receiver of the inserted belief systems is never conscious of the insertions nor ever questions it.

These systems bond us together, assure our commonality, and give us a feeling of security and stability. The entire culture accepts the belief system and passes it on as a fact to each new generation.

In certain families, the children understand they will attend college to study law, medicine, or music. Other children know before high school that they will work in the local factory. Other examples are religion and politics. Cultural belief systems have more roots than weeds and are harder to uproot.

Rebels and Visionaries

Society's rebels are most interesting. Despite every effort of the family, religion, and society to insert belief systems, rebels refuse to accept the belief system insertions. In disgust, society discards them.

As a result, they have fewer restricting belief systems. With more conscious mind to work with, they produce creative and unusual ideas, and some are very successful.

A Visionary seldom has suffered a normal education. By that, I mean our present "keep the status quo" education systems. Somehow, someway, the system did not bludgeon him with the normal heavy cover of belief systems.

The status quo people considers a visionary, a threatening mortal infection, a dangerous "loose cannon" to be feared and destroyed by any means possible. They would rather have root canal surgery without anesthesia than let a visionary in their life!

Belief Systems Can Block Biological Urges

A man can create a belief system that he is impotent. But at night, while dreaming, he will function normally. Remove the belief system and the problem will disappear.

Belief systems can create unbearable pressure--emotional and physical. A belief system that blocks a basic biological urge will cause grave psychological problems. The body will seek relief through any remedy: drugs, alcohol, fast cars, even pain.

Your belief systems screen whether you can allow sexual satisfaction to occur or not to occur. For instance: a belief system is inserted saying that sex is fine under certain conditions. People of the same race, age, religion, approximate height, or weight, same or opposite sex, or only if married.

A second one is inserted saying that it is natural not to desire sex except as proscribed by the first. A third is inserted saying that if you violate one and two, you feel guilty and "go to hell." A fourth belief system is inserted that says there is no such things as a belief system and the ball game is over.

Belief Systems:
1. Tend To Create What You Know Over And Over
2. Create Familiarity

People react to what happens to them. When a reaction handles the experience and they survive, a belief system is established. Each variation of the experience expands the belief system.

From then on, every time a similar experience happens, they unconsciously operate out of the past belief system instead of reality.

Some are obvious, while most are not. These triggers can be hourly, daily, weekly, monthly, yearly, or once every decade.

For example, little boys and little girls learn how to relate to their mothers and fathers to get what they want. The little boy's belief systems about how to relate to his mother expands to include relating to all women including his wife. The girls duplicate this behavior with men. Sometimes the belief systems for relating to mother and father merge and they relate to all people from one expanded belief system.

These belief systems do not work as well in adult life as in childhood; but the belief systems will continue until death, with all parties never quite figuring out why nothing much totally worked in their lives.

Once a belief system is formed, you must operate inside it or you will suffer anxiety. Anxiety is the most painful experience you can have and people will avoid it at any cost.

When we operate inside our belief systems, we experience familiarity which does not create anxiety. We seek familiarity to avoid anxiety.

A miserable childhood will create belief systems that in order to survive, one must be miserable. Misery becomes familiar. Fun and pleasure, the absence of misery, can be desired but when received, create anxiety. To avoid the painful anxiety, the person will create misery to attain familiarity.

Such belief systems are difficult to understand since none of us, to our conscious knowledge, seek pain and misery. However, the game is played at the unconscious level.

There is no bizarre behavior today that couldn't be explained if we had a copy of the past experiences and the consequent belief systems that a person developed to handle them. All behavior including bizarre behavior is a belief system fulfilling itself to avoid anxiety.

Examples

A girl constantly abused by her father develops a pattern of belief systems to handle it. If by chance she marries a man who treats her kindly, she will experience anxiety and irritate her husband until he abuses her. She will never figure out she created the male abuse to establish a familiar situation and thus relieve the anxiety. She will say, "all men abuse women."

People go crazy trying to please someone so they can gain that person's love and approval. Being pleasing for a person who is used to experiencing rejection, can induce anxiety. This person may even do something bizarre to avoid anxiety and create the familiar sadness which comes from rejection.

A man raised without love and approval will marry a woman who cannot give him love and approval. Both will avoid love and approval of each other, but say they desire it. They will stay together in misery, but not anxiety. They will snarl at each other for a lifetime and create identical behavior in their offspring who will marry and pass it on to the next generation.

Likewise, if a person who has been overweight all of his or her life were to become thin, incredible anxiety would occur. Unless the belief system patterns about the early eating patterns can be discovered and eliminated, the person will allow the lost weight to return to avoid anxiety.

Unless you uncover the underlying patterns of belief systems from which you operate, your behaviors will remain set in concrete. You will create the exact past behavior over and over. This is true for a person, a group, a city, a nation, our universe.

Whether you are happy, selfish, or greedy is programmed before you reach age 10. You will mostly be like your parents.

Here is a horrible but very typical example of how destructive a belief system can be.

Alexandra is lovely, middle-aged, divorced, and childless. All she can remember her whole life is that she <u>never</u> wanted to live alone. She has had many boyfriends and spends every night attending any activity to avoid being alone.

Why can't she connect to a loving, meaningful relationship? She desires this in every conscious cell in her body. The problem is that she has an unconscious belief system that says, "In order to survive, you have to be alone."

Alexandra was an abused child, constantly punished, and left alone. She remembers as a child being alone and feeling alone. And she survived! The first belief system formed at the <u>level of survival</u> was, "I am alone and I survived; therefore, to survive, I must be alone!" This belief system was reinforced everyday of her young, before memory life.

No matter how much she wants to be with someone, in order to survive, avoid anxiety and create familiarity, she has to be alone. This core belief system will not allow any other life.

A thunderbolt cannot overcome the cumulative power of daily insertions over time. All of us are controlled this way.

You cannot have what you presently want because the belief system keeping you from what you want was inserted earlier and deeper than your present desire.

Belief Systems Automatically Create Your Destiny

Life is an endless path of opportunities hidden by belief systems. Every person gets many opportunities in life to be successful, but belief systems prevent us from realizing them.

If you have a belief system that says you are a superior person, as well as being wealthy, healthy, and wise, you will become that type of person.

The rich get richer and the poor get poorer because of belief systems. A child who has a rich father observed and self-inserted belief systems about being rich. The same for the child of a poor father.

How can a ghetto person believe he can learn, when every person he observed or talked with had negative belief systems about minorities and conveyed it to him everyday of his life. "In order to survive, I have to fail and feel worthless."

This belief system is buried deep in the person at a very young and impressionable age. He has observed scores of people failing, feeling worthless and surviving. What are the chances of operating out of positive belief systems under these conditions.

However, if this person had lived his whole life with crippled, blind, and deaf people who had no belief systems about blind, crippled and deaf people, he too would not have any! The whole mess of belief systems was inserted!

There are lots of happy blind, deaf, and crippled people. Some of the happiest people I have ever met were handicapped people. Because these people are blind and deaf, society cannot insert the destructive belief systems that create the misery. It is we that have a belief system about handicapped people.

The problem is not the condition under which you live but the belief systems about the conditions under which you live. Many people who live in miserable conditions are very happy, others are not. Until I discovered belief systems, I could not understand this.

Intelligence is being free of unconscious belief systems. Some people happen to be burdened with restrictive belief systems that hamper their gifts from developing. A person is made to feel stupid by his or her belief systems.

We are all operating below our potential. Every time we failed in school, at work, or socially, and survived, we created a limiting belief system: "The way to survive is to fail."

A person who has a belief system that he is a failure will only allow himself to see opportunities to fail. If you have a belief system that says you cannot learn math, you will not learn math. If you have a belief system that says you are just an average person, that's your destiny.

Ninety-nine percent of the million or billion belief systems we have are confirming or a combination of original belief systems. About twenty percent of those belief systems control much of our daily behavior. And we operate constantly out of two or three.

Viewpoints, Convictions, Truths, and Moods

When we observe people doing or saying something, and everybody appears to be agreeing with it, we form a belief system that it is a truth.

Do you have a viewpoint? Belief systems have created every one of your points of view and they will stay with you until death, unless you can find the original event and reexperience it.

Belief systems cause people to have concrete convictions about subjects they know little about and have absolutely no idea how to support. For instance, God.

People have told me what God wants, what He thinks, what He dislikes, and for which activities He will punish me. Yet, I have never met anyone who has met God!

Did you ever do something that seemed absolutely right, but now you can't understand how you could have felt so certain at that time? You can have opposite viewpoints and operate from each one on different days. "Look before you leap." "To hesitate is to be lost."

What is your belief system about being poor, overweight, thin, in poor health, lazy, rich, loving, guilty, an atheist, an agnostic ,waking up sad, frustrated, defeated, helpless, hopeless,the day of judgement, the golden rule, life's meaning?

Any mood or attitude is a belief system. We are full of unreasonable expectations created by inserted belief systems; and when the expectations are not realized, we feel miserable. Friday nights are for fun. Saturday nights are for dates, etc. If that doesn't happen, we end up unhappy.

Fire fighters report that people who have been awakened naked in bed by fire, have chosen to die of smoke inhalation next to an exit door, rather than expose themselves. Because of a belief system about nakedness, these people chose death over life. Shame of our bodies is a belief system. You didn't have it when you were born.

The French Academy in 1772, after careful study, declared

that no stones could fall from the sky, because there are no stones in the sky. As a result, all the museums threw away their meteorite specimens.   We may have similar situations in the present regarding UFO's.

Painful Doing

When you do something socially acceptable that you didn't like doing, it's likely that you have a belief system that says you will lose love or approval if you don't do it.

When you do what you don't want to do, you get angry. Anger not expressed becomes resentment, not expressed becomes depression, not expressed becomes disease and death. Therefore, by doing what you don't want to do, you give up vitality. Ultimately, you give up your life. It is a form of misery. What do you hate doing? Why do you continue doing it.?

Belief Systems and Prejudice

What credit do I take for being white? It just happened that way! What credit do I deserve? None! What benefits? None! But I have a belief system that says I'm superior. I don't even know I have it. If I knew I had it, I would have no idea where I got it. If confronted, I would probably deny its existence.

We don't have belief systems about an animal's color. We own black, white and brown dogs but only have white friends? No matter what color a cow is, the milk is the same. When a black and white child meet to play, both have to pierce and overcome accumulated passed on belief systems from parents, peers, and other authority figures.

If we are separated by belief systems, then we are indeed a curious and strange race.

Belief Systems, Pain, Lies and Violence

We could not, as conscious human beings, tolerate the evil conditions that exist in the world today nor let it happen without belief systems.

We have belief systems about TV and newspapers. The belief system states that reporters exaggerate and sensationalize the news. We read about terrible deaths, bombings, kidnapping, millions starve in Africa. We watch war on TV. It's not a movie, but the real thing! If we witnessed it personally, we would be full of emotion.

Most of us feel that the people who watched the gladiators fight and die must have been really sick. Yet, we eagerly wait for a championship fight where two people will batter each other's brains into senselessness. We "make believe" so we do not have to know because to know is to feel, to suffer, to act.

What kind of culture derives pleasure from pain? What is the difference between an injury on the football field and one on the field of battle? Every Sunday, people maim each other playing football. All injuries are subject to replays during the game and again on the evening news.

Without belief systems, football injuries would be unbearably painful to watch! Perhaps an electronic wizard could wire the nervous systems of the football players to our bodies through the set. Then we could feel the pain. I wonder how many people would turn their sets on.

Belief Systems, Job Descriptions, and Titles

Belief systems create job descriptions and different personalities in the same person at different times and circumstances. Your boss will have a different personality on the golf course, at work with the boys, and at church with his family and so will you. We all have belief systems about how a mother, father, wife, lover, and friend should behave according to specific activities. Each situation and each personality operates out of different belief systems.

Type A behavior is a group of belief systems. It's salient characteristics are:

1. Compelling sense of time.
2. Urgency.
3. Aggressiveness.
4. Competitiveness.
5. Free floating hostility.

All five are inserted belief systems. No one is born with the above. Remove them and type A behavior will disappear. Type A behavior is closely linked to heart attacks.

There are people in this world that are underemployed. That is, they are over-educated and over-qualified for their job. Belief systems about job titles keep them poor.

People like this cannot take a high-paying job as a plumber. If they do, they become anxious and uncomfortable. These people choose low-paying jobs with fancy titles rather than take higher-paying positions that don't pump up their self-esteem.

This frozen mental waste could be melted by removing blocking belief systems. Their whole life could be turned around.

Friendship and Expectation

Unconscious belief systems are secrets we keep from ourselves, but other people, may spot them. People relate to you by adjusting to your belief systems. Friendships become combinations and acceptances of each person's different belief systems.

When we introduce ourselves to other people, it is our belief systems that we are introducing and merging. When we argue, we are debating the differences in our belief systems. When we don't know what to do, it's because we don't have a belief system in that area.

Belief Systems and Sexual Encounters

Young girls in love are deeply afraid to go to bed with the young man of their dreams. Every cell in their body is wary of it. Why are women afraid? Why do men demand it?

Unconscious belief systems about sex and love are confusing to men and women in love. The confusion comes from thousands of unconscious inserted contradicting belief systems regarding Mother, Father, God, The Virgin Mary, Venus, whores, sex, hell, macho men, and folklore.

Young men demand proof of love through sexual encounters. A man must be sure. Who wants to raise other men's children and play the fool? Women who agree to show proof of love are then subjected to abuse by the men who suggested the arrangement.

A man may have the following belief systems: If my girl loves me, she will prove it by having sex with me. If she has sex with me, she's a whore and I can't love or marry a whore. Furthermore, the Virgin Mary didn't have sexual encounters, neither does my Mother or any other nice person. Both are bewildered by the event.

The sexual encounter could leave a feeling of resentment, hate, and guilt lasting a lifetime.

In primitive times, women operated in a male-dominated world and predicting man's behavior was essential to survival. Women have less upper body strength than men. Strength was important, not facts or brains. Many belief systems passed down through unconscious observation from this era can still be activated.

Status Quo belief systems are set up to create misery for people who try to live outside them. Although the initial sexual encounters are stressful and confusing, no help will ever be available because the belief systems are unconscious so nothing can be done.

For example:

Two people can't get married because of belief systems about religion. There's a commercial reason for this. Neither religion wants to lose a repeat customer and his offspring for centuries. This authority is just trying to hold on to its constituency. You can find similar belief systems in politics and other groups.

We all know and possibly experienced the guilt from living in sin before marriage. Then we get married and tell our offspring not to... We unconsciously verify as valid both belief systems. We practice birth control but never think about it. We tell our children not to. A child is told sex is bad for them and discovers that his own parents do it!

Number of Belief Systems

How many belief systems do you have? The mind is capable of creating several belief systems each second. There are one billion seconds in 32 years. Trillions of belief system overlap, connect, interrelate, and reinforce each other. Belief systems are everywhere. You operate out of them all the time.

Incorrect Belief Systems

Back in the second century, Claudius Ptolemy said everything including the sun, planets, and stars, revolved around a stationary earth. Everybody accepted this idea, including the clergy. Like so many belief systems, it acquired the status of accepted wisdom. The theory was beautiful; and everybody wanted to believe it. So, it became a fact!

In a world of uncertainty we constantly feel hopeless, helpless, and powerless; we all need something solid to hold on to. We need facts. A fact makes you feel secure and that feels good. Naturally, the earth on which we lived was the center of everything. How very nice and convenient. And God was just out there beyond the clouds.

Nicholas Copernicus came along and said the earth was not the center of the universe. He stated the earth revolved around the sun and so did the planets. His theory pushed the stars so far away, that a new belief system had to be created for where God and heaven dwelt.

This is not a funny situation to people who are in the belief system business. The clergy resented having to move God, so they resisted the idea; and as a result, it took a century to filter down to the common folk and penetrate the accepted belief systems.

Spending hundreds of years passing along an incorrect belief system seems like a terrible waste. However, right now, we have trillions of unconscious, unverified belief systems that we are passing along to the next generation.

These include belief systems about matter and energy that quantum physics have proven as wrong as the belief systems that said the earth was flat or the center of the universe! Worst, however, on a personal level are belief systems each one of us are passing on unconsciously to the next generation.

By our example and through their observation, we tell them that alcohol, cigarettes, drugs, sugar, salt, overeating, war, poverty, overpopulation, selfishness, greed--you name it--are okay; and we are no more conscious of this than the people who believed the earth was flat.

Belief System Blame

Who is to blame for the belief systems that were inserted against our will before we were able to choose? How do we get even?

The obvious answer is your parents. They did it to you, but in all fairness, it was done to them and to their parents. Follow this logic to its conclusion and you'll end up needing to get even with Adam and Eve and then God. (Is Adam and Eve a belief system too? How about God?)

Getting even is a belief system. Get rid of it. Give yourself a break and forgive everybody everywhere and be thankful you broke through the cultural trance that mentally enslaved your ancestors since time started. This includes your favorite and non-favorite people, all the Popes, Rabbis, Villains, and Saints. You will feel great. (See Chapter 15, Major Upset Belief Systems: Forgiveness, Page 172)

Pure Life Equals Consciousness

Pure life is pure consciousness, right here and now. It is all the times you are being aware of when you lock the door, kiss a baby, hug a love one, etc. It is a place of boundless energy.

Imagine consciousness as pure white light.

We are born seeing pure white light. Then:

Before memory, Our Father, Mother, Society, Friends, Tradition, Race, etc, lays its red, blue, black, brown, green, yellow, belief system filters on us. What is the chance of ever seeing white light again? You have to see what color life is now and start removing the belief system filters.

Death as well as birth is part of the overall cosmic art of pure life. Between birth and death, your life was meant for pure life (i.e. expanding consciousness).therefore, a PURE life will be all events consciously experienced.

Belief System Enlargement

When civilized man first desired to cross a river, he chose the most narrow part of the river. Later, he created a floating structure to accomplish this task (ferry). Gradually, all of the roads led to the ferry. When man then invented the bridge, it was built where the ferry crossed the river because that's where all the roads were already. It probably wasn't the best place to build the bridge. The bridge, not only handles the earlier floating traffic, but also the new traffic.

The growth of a belief system is similar to this. Whenever a belief system is not able to keep you unconscious and automatic, the ego creates a bigger one which encompasses all similarly related ones. The new belief system handles the past and the future.

For example, a person has an unconscious belief system for each of the following:

Feeling	Reaction
anxiety	smoke
worry	drink alcohol
fear	sweat
pain	shake
anger	yell

The ego may decide to combine these belief system under, "Whenever I'm ill at ease, I will drink, smoke, sweat, shake, and yell." This enlarged belief system includes the above and will ultimately also include every other situation you could experience under the feeling, "ill at ease."

Ultimately, ill at ease will merge with a "whenever I'm miserable" belief system. Since the ego does all this at your unconscious level, you never get to decide. Layer upon layer of belief systems accumulate over your lifetime like the falling leaves in the forest over many autumns.

Soon, you can't tell one leaf from another. It's all just one big carpet of leaves or one huge overriding unconscious belief system. Except for flashes of consciousness, you live on automatic, unknowing of your behavior.

Here is another variation: I drink too much because I have a belief system that was self-inserted that says, when I feel down or low in spirits, drinking will pick me up. (Similar to smoking insertion.) However, when I drink too much, I feel bad and I have a belief system that says when I feel bad, I am bad.

Furthermore, I have a belief system that says when I am bad, I should be punished. When you are an adult, how do you punish yourself? By doing what was familiar as a child? (How did your parents punish you?) If I was sent to bed without a meal as a child, I will starve myself as an adult. Ultimately, I get to be miserable.

Conversely, when you can discover and eliminate parts of a major belief system, the ego is forced to decrease or lessen its automatic behavior grip on the person. You can force a collapse of a big unconscious belief system into a smaller one.

If each of us accomplishes the rooting out of a major belief system, our collective UNconscious will shrink, while our collective consciousness will increase.

Our Present Operating System

If you view a town or a city from a small plane its obvious you could have designed it better. Of course you have the advantage of a clean start.

The town was created by primitive people with immediate but completely different objectives in mind, who had no idea they were building a city.

You might say that all our towns and cities were designed by primitive people on foot to be used by modern people using cars and airplanes. Our brain is a modern highway supported by a past of footpath belief systems.

Our belief systems were formed by a primitive man that more resembles an animal than what we have evolved to be. We are operating our lives with belief systems who's origins are in the limbic animal area of the brain that have been passed down to us by observation, unconsciously over 10,000 years and we are not aware of their existence.

In the town above, suppose you had a magic wand and could move or eliminate not only the paths and rivers, but the town itself. When you eliminate or neutralize a belief system, that's what happens to you.

Controlling Positive and Negative Belief Systems
Until They Can Be Discovered and Eliminated

"You got to bring joy up to the maximum, you got to bring gloom down to the minimum, and don't mess with Mr. In-Between." When I was a boy, this was a popular song on the radio. When I asked grown ups how to do the above, they said: "It's just a song."

The way to bring about the song's goal is to get control of

your belief systems until you can eliminate them. You can't discover and eliminate all of them at once. Here is a suggestion on how to handle belief systems until then.

The belief system controls the situation.

Our egos are automatic and have millions of initial and confirming belief systems of all sorts and flavors. It will always recall or bring up similar or identical past belief systems.

Pessimism is a belief system that says, "In order to survive, bad things have to happen to me." If bad is familiar to you, you will create bad all around you. If bad things do not happen, you will suffer anxiety until you make something bad happen.

A negative belief system will confirm itself by remembering only those past incidences that agree with the belief, "To survive bad things have to happen" and the mind brings up all the past (belief system) events that proves the person bad.

If you are sick, the ego will search and find a belief system that says you are not a healthy person. Stop it! Start remembering all the times you felt terrific.

Optimism is a belief system that says: "In order to survive, good things will happen to me, everything and everybody around me."

Instead of asking why do I always fail, ask why do I always succeed? The latter sentence will also confirm itself and bring up all the past memories of when you did succeed.

Be optimistic! Expect good things to happen. Look for evidence that it is happening. Magnify your desire over and over. Never doubt it, just expect it to happen. Act like it is happening. Prove it to yourself by finding concrete examples in the present that confirm that your future is happening. Believe it and it will happen.

By asking positive questions, your positive belief systems about your past will bring up positive memories to confirm. You will believe positive things will happen to you <u>and they will</u>! You always reflect your belief systems. You can create your future by directing your belief systems.

Look out for unconscious negatives, "Bless me Father, I have sinned." Instead, "Bless me Father, I have maintained positive belief systems all week as follows:...."

I have supported my family and myself.
I have lived within the law.
I have loved and supported my wife, children and parents.
I have done my best to live a wholesome life.
I report to work promptly and give fair value for what I earn.

How do we use this knowledge?

Spend ten minutes each day writing down all you have done right. We are all programmed to notice what is wrong with us, but 99% of what we are is right. Why not appreciate yourself?

Change the way you view life. For example, people sometimes ask me where I go on vacation. I tell them Washington, D.C. I had a beautiful place to stay. I got up late, gained a tan, visited friends, stayed out late, and woke up whenever I wanted. Best vacation I ever had. People tell me how lucky I am. I agree. We all have great belief systems about Washington, D.C. However, the best part was that I did not have to pack and unpack, endure airplanes, taxis, and strange living arrangements or their expense. You see, I live in Washington, D.C.

Another person who had a belief system that staying home during a vacation was the pits, would have had a terrible time. The belief system controls the situation. Changing your programming to "like what you get" makes tremendous joy available to you.

As you develop good belief systems in one area of your life, they will tend to overflow into other areas. A person who is a good athlete has belief systems that help in creating his athletic abilities. Because he feels good about his athletic abilities, he will create belief systems that he is attractive to the opposite sex, that people like him, and so on.

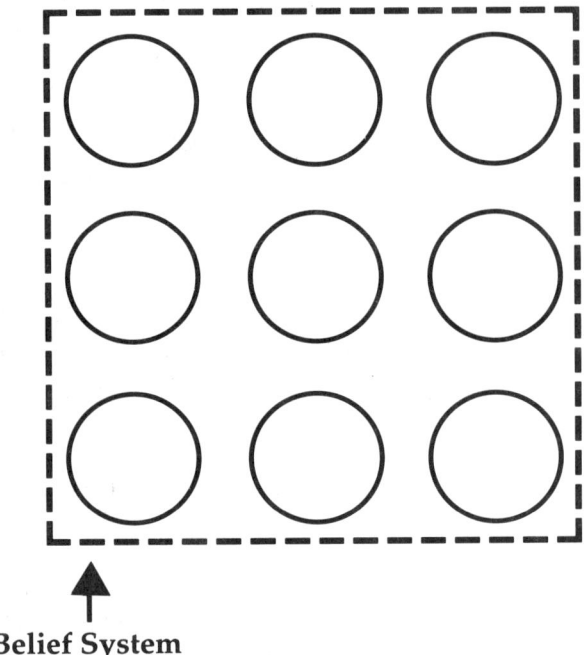

Belief System

You cannot solve this puzzle because you have a belief system that there is an imaginary line around the dots.

See page 66 for solution

Chapter 5

INFANTS AND CHILDREN

Why do we like infants so much?

A child is full of joy, interest, excitement, fun, happiness, anticipation, desire, and eagerness. They are enthusiastic and vital. They want it all now! Yesterday and tomorrow does not exist for them. To a two year old, an hour is a long time. A week of waiting for something is almost unbearable. A month is longer than forever.

Babies are never bored. They want to touch and feel everything. What they touch and feel is internalized directly. There is no blocking belief systems. For them, life is a ball, we are all the same, and all they want are more new fun experiences.

An infant is as close to consciousness as you can get. The more conscious you are, the better you feel. Does an infant worry, suffer guilt, or become anxious? No. Consciousness does not know these things.

We enjoy watching their behavior even though we can no longer imitate it.

The infant that puts one block upon another has made a connection as great as Handel did in putting parts of music together. Handel would experience ecstasy and notice it because it would penetrate accumulated layers of belief systems. To the child, it is just another ho-hum ecstasy, because without belief systems, every experience is ecstasy.

Put infants of different status, creed, races, together and they play their hearts out. Ten years later, they will feel awkward, but not know why. When they are teenagers, it will not be possible to bring them together because the accumulated layers of passed on belief systems from parents, peers, and authority figures will be too difficult for consciousness to pierce.

A Child's Mind

The world's most valuable asset is a child's mind and it is absolutely helpless against belief system insertion in the early stages before it is able to gain self-confidence, perspective, judgement, and make distinctions.

Every child starts out a genius. As the child grows, consciousness is covered by belief systems. Except for flashes of consciousness, the child will lose vitality throughout life.

From birth on, we expose this delightful, happy, content, and defenseless child to teachers and adults who are completely on "automatic" themselves. They are unconsciously programmed to believe that criticism, pain, fear, guilt, worry, anxiety, and punishment without explanation, are good ways to teach and raise children.

Children believe what their elders (parents, relatives and teachers) say as they insert the accepted unverified belief systems about religion, sex, rain, snow, skin color, sports, nationalities, occupations, food, music, and who to love and hate. There is no way for a child to resist these insertions which are entwined in the fabric of language, attitudes, and religious rituals.

Spontaneity is wiped out, natural traits are distorted. Strength may be described as aggression, rebellion, solitude or macho-ism depending on the mentor's belief systems.

All parts of the mind will be blunted. Intelligence, intuition, creativity, imagination, insight and belief systems will be created that induce them to believe they never possessed any of these gifts. Before we are one hour old, we probably have thousands of belief systems about air, blankets, cribs, people, voices, warm bodies, and breasts, that we will control us until death.

As a child, we look around and see everything that "really is", but we somehow don't fit like others. We get anxious.

Children are told they cannot know and yet they survive. Therefore, to survive, they must not know. Thereafter, the child relies on others. He conforms, does not think, no longer trusts his own senses, and eventually ignores his own experiences. "What is" becomes "What ain't". Continue this every minute of every day. Soon, layer upon layer of belief systems form a dizzying, confusing, bewildering, impossible to understand puzzle to the child.

All too quickly, the child is operating automatically out of his "drilled-in" belief systems and cannot make conscious choices. The basis is set for accepting more and more conditioning belief systems.

Gradually, children learn to see only what other adults see. No one tells them there is more. How can they? They don't perceive any more themselves. If you still see it, they will tell you it doesn't exist.

The more you see the way others see, the more you will "fit", get love and approval, and avoid anxiety.

Each time a child does some innocent thing that upsets one of our belief systems, we frown, and in some way, insert a similar belief system in the child. If you are rude, kind, prompt, late, obedient or disobedient, play fair or unfair, the child will echo it. Soon the child has the same belief systems as the status quo does.

How often do we observe a child told to choose whatever

he wants to be, but then told to be a good boy like Johnny. Being like Johnny is a restrictive belief system. The implication is that if the child becomes like Johnny, he will receive motherly love. If not, desolation! The child is told there is no pressure, yet feels it all the time.

By unconscious observation, these insertions will pass to future generations. Not only your belief systems, but all those people who have power over the child: any older child, relatives, teachers, religious leaders, Batman and Robin, as well as Superman, and he will expand and adjust them as needed.

The ultimate source of all these belief systems is our ancestors; and they believed the earth was flat!

The Learning Process

These inserted belief systems stop <u>active</u> learning and the <u>passive</u> learning of being told "what to see" begins.

Parents and other status quo adults decide the delightful, happy self-exploring child is now ready to respond to "formal" teaching.

Follow these children and watch as their vitality lessens!

Children are taught to accept facts and ideas by teachers and adults who were destroyed by the same programming.

In elementary school, all the children learn all the subjects: music, math, English. Children readily spell Triskaidekaphobia. At this time, they are completely spontaneous and can instantly display any emotion without the guilt or fear of peer disapproval. None will die that way.

Belief systems will accumulate in them until they join the living dead.

The Education Factory

The education system is like a factory. Enter at six and get programmed. All children aren't ready to be programmed. The damage is awesome. Children that fall behind develop belief systems that say they are inadequate in, what have you, math, English, science, and avoid those subjects the rest of their lives.

Children who fall ill during the school year return and can never catch up creating similar, destructive belief systems. Children with learning disabilities are destroyed before help arrives.

All education should be individually self-paced.

Art instructs as well as pleases. A six year old viewing a movie about blacks living in hovels and singing happily on their way to 16 hours of hard labor in sun drenched cotton fields would walk away with a belief system that slavery was a lot of fun for black people. Once inserted, that belief is there until death.

Once the belief systems are inserted, they are never questioned and continually reinforced. Their children like a ventriloquist's dummy, will play back similar messages for their children.

Punishment

Forcing a child to do a task as punishment can create a belief system that work is punishment. Try to earn a living and be successful with that kind of belief system! Every time you go to work, you feel you are being punished.

A child about to be punished experiences absolute and total terror. From a child's perception, he is small, helpless, and powerless. His parents are larger and powerful. He sees only the visible anger in his parents' eyes. He is completely dependent for love and all life's necessities on the very people about to punish him. There are few, if any, previous experiences to relate to, or evaluate the coming punishment, thus it's total panic.

Few adults, never mind children, would understand the pain of punishment as part of an overall loving intention. The punishment is perceived by the child as an unloving act and rejection.

The result: intense consciousness with total perception concentrated on the pain, the terror, and the absence of love. No one witnessing the event could correctly identify the "near death" intensity of the feelings and emotions or how the child interpreted the total event to form the belief systems. But the child will survive the incident and create one or more belief systems. For instance:

1. Whenever I want attention, be bad.
2. In order to survive, I have to be punished.
3. Whenever people love you, they punish you.
4. Pain and love are inseparable.
5. Big people hurt little people.
6. Little people are powerless and helpless.
7. Love is terrifying.
8. All the above and more.

Therefore, when in the future, we experience feelings or emotions similar to our original experience, it is not the present experience we experience, rather we trigger the original panic. This explains why our upset is so out of proportion to the present situation. We lose consciousness, we neither evaluate nor relate, we just relive the panic and terror of the original incident.

When we calm down, we realize we have over reacted, but its too late. The yelling, the shouting, the insults and physical damage to ourselves and others has already occurred. Most of the time, we just don't realize why we react certain ways at certain times. It is a mystery to us.

Teenagers

It is impossible to estimate how many belief systems and combinations of belief systems we have formed by the time we are teenagers.

Teenagers are very vulnerable. They have not learned how to ease the pain and humiliation of their naked need for peer love and approval and, thus, will accept any belief system.

How ridiculous and pathetic all this is since a teenager's peers are equally crippled by belief systems, and gaining their acceptance and approval is useless! Teenagers are all alike. They do the same things, like the same things, yet within this narrow sliver of remaining life, try to be different. Most teenagers have lost 95% of their ability to be a conscious person.

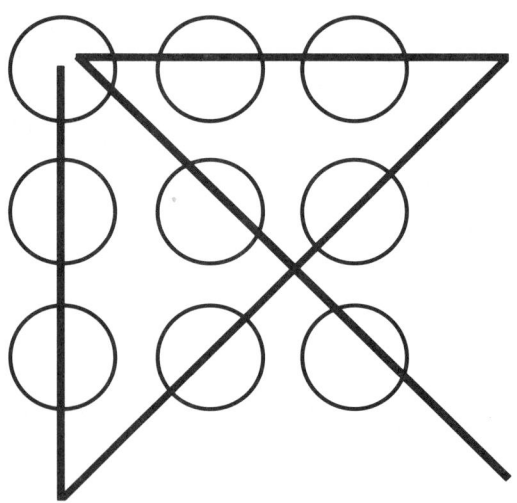

As soon as you eliminate the belief system,
a solution appears.

See Page __67__

Belief System

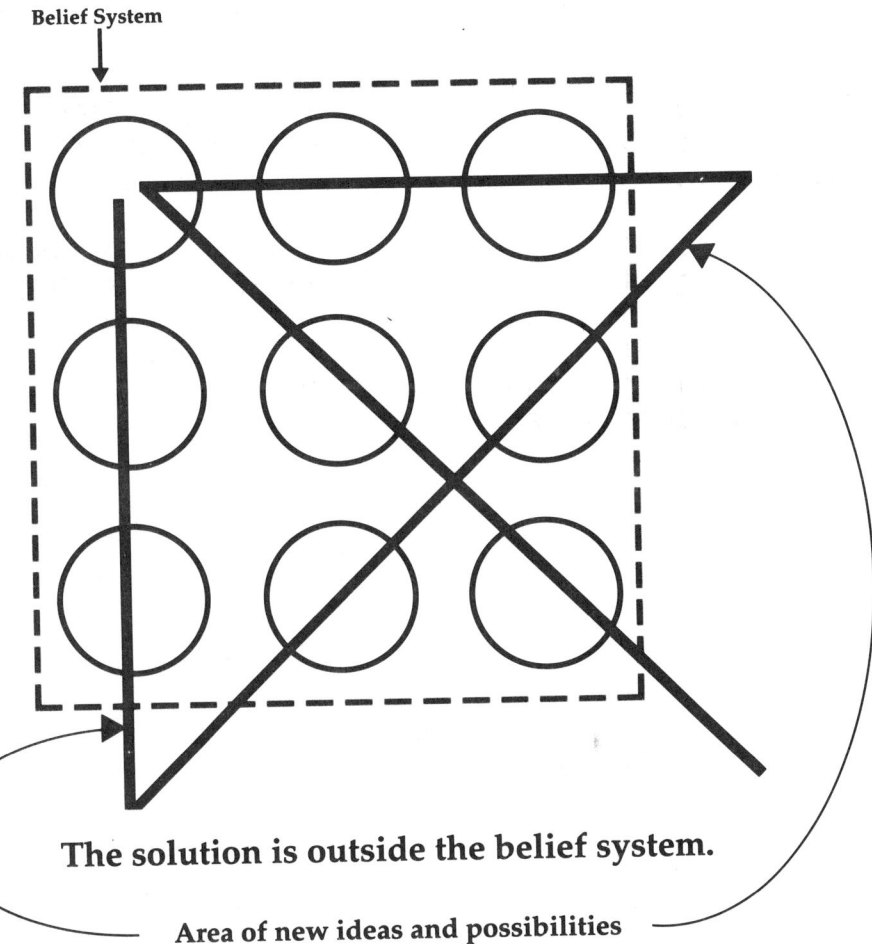

The solution is outside the belief system.

Area of new ideas and possibilities

Chapter 6

WHY OLD AND YOUNG PEOPLE DRIFT APART

We cannot understand our ancestors and their actions because they created different belief systems based upon their experiences. The same is true with our own children and our children's children. We drift apart because of our different and unconscious belief systems formed from different experiences.

Everybody's belief systems are as individual as fingerprints. Young and old people have a belief system about Joe DiMaggio. Children know him as,"Mr. Coffee". Old people know him as the"Yankee Clipper." Is Roy Rogers a cowboy or a restaurant? We are unable to communicate from one generation to another because our belief systems are from different times and experiences.

Belief systems lock us into frozen identities. To each person that knows us, we are whatever their belief systems say we are. Your teachers' belief systems about you are from the time period of their experience of you. Your sister may hear from all her friends what a wonderful person you are. However, to her you are the rotten brother from her youth. Only the people who met you recently have the most up to date complete belief system of who you are. And the same is true of you regarding your past and present friends. "You can never be a hero in your own hometown," makes much more sense from this context.

When you go to your 25th high school reunion and run out of subjects to talk about with your old friends, it is because you are operating out of different belief systems from different experiences.

You may say you do not like the way people relate to you. Yet their actions do not create anxiety. If it did, you would change your behavior. Your unconscious controls all.

Parents And Children

Parents want their children to love and care for them. A phone call would be nice. Old people cannot understand why they feel and often times are neglected by their children. They have a belief system that says their children should not neglect them.

It is not an accident, or unfortunate circumstance, how your children relate to you. It is a reflection of their belief systems.

The belief system that says, "In order to survive, take care of your parents," was not inserted. Years later, out of desperation, parents try to insert this belief system by using guilt. However, since the most effective and successful belief systems are inserted early before memory and ability to integrate is present, the effort is less than successful.

The result is, parents are still neglected most of the time and the children feel guilty all the time.

The inserted childhood belief systems will determine if the children will call, care, and love their aging parents. (Take care of your parents and your children will observe it.)

Old People and Prices

Grown children are driven crazy by their parents' refusal to buy the proper food and clothing for themselves, even though they have ample funds. The older people will not buy because the price is too high according to their belief systems.

People develop belief systems about prices during the years

when they are in charge of buying for themselves and their family. All prices in the future are related to the belief systems established during this time.

Old People and Age

Do we have a collective belief system that says aging means a decline in health? One hundred years ago, sixty was old age. This belief system was inserted in each succeeding generation; and even though there are people seventy years old playing racquetball and tennis, we still act like sixty is old age. Many of us believe aging means decline in health and body, so we decline.

When we get sick we lose interest in social and physical activities, but we don't get upset because we know why. During the recovery phase, we forget we are recovering and tell ourselves (belief system) that we feel bad because we are getting old. That feeling tired is normal. The result is less enthusiasm and resigned feelings of inevitable decline. We believe we should decline so we do. When we realize we are operating out of a belief system we get better immediately.

Old People and the Good Old Days

A lot of people hold onto belief systems about how great the good old days were. How dumb can we be!

The old days may have had lower prices and things were simpler. However, nobody, given a choice between now and then, would choose the good old days.

Thousands of people were employed in New York City alone to clean up after horses. There was no central heating, hot water, or indoor plumbing. How about unpasteurized milk, apples with worms, fruit in the summer months only, no penicillin or other wonder drugs?

A good employee in a good company made 12 dollars a week working twelve hours a day six days a week. He might live to 40 or 50 years of age, if illness or accident did not claim him first. A doctor made about $1,000 a year.

Almost everybody was in debt, broke, and poor. Few people were able to save any money for retirement. No welfare or medical plans existed. The good old days were awful!

Old People and Grandchildren

Loving grandchildren is easy because we have no belief systems in this area.

At birth, our hearts are open, but as we grow and offer love to everyone, we insert restrictive belief systems about giving and receiving love because rejection hurts. We hurt ourselves and others. Our hearts close down for safety's sake. The result is a huge backlog of compacted love.

A baby does not reject or frighten us. It doesn't trigger belief systems about hurt, anger, distrust and betrayal, It just creates a safe place to release love.   Consequently, this backlog of compacted love rushes out through this hole in our love armor. When a baby comes, we love the baby the way we would love everybody except for the self inserted belief systems. Unfortunately, as the child grows, we insert the belief systems in them decreasing the love and vitality.

The End Result

From the moment of birth, belief systems start to dilute our spontaneity. Nothing is new or exciting, nothing changes, it's all the same. If you don't believe me, visit an old person in their home, or if you have the guts, a home for the aged!

Most old people are bored most of the time. Waiting is what their lives are all about. You name it, they are waiting for it. A check in the mail, a bus, a meeting, a telephone or visit from their children, etc. Mostly, they are waiting to die.

What happened to these people between birth and death? Belief systems took away the "now;" they took away the vitality. They took away the joy of conscious life. Perhaps it's possible to determine when a person will die by how bored they are, or how well they wait for things.

Be Miserable Tree

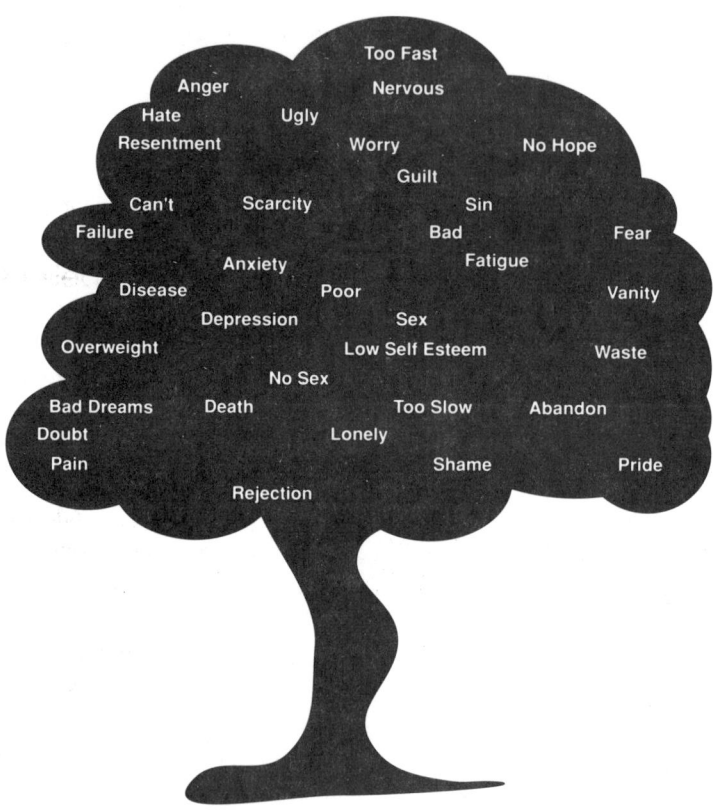

**In order to survive,
I must be miserable.**

Chapter 7

IN ORDER TO SURVIVE, YOU HAVE TO BE MISERABLE

The primary goal of every living thing is to survive. Surviving is a trial and error procedure. If you do or feel something, and survive, a belief system is formed. (I eat and survive. Therefore, to survive I must eat.)

The first belief system formed becomes a core or controlling belief system. By repeating the initial action in various circumstances, you form different combinations of belief systems that become part of and group with the core belief system.

Every time you worry and survive you also form belief systems that group together. If you eat and worry at the same time they will combine. The more you do some particular thing, the more belief systems you have in that area. Belief systems gather around common themes and tend to group together. Many belief systems support other belief systems, with all belief systems supporting the core belief system.

All these core belief systems also group together to form a master survival belief system which is "In order to survive, you have to be miserable." *Everything you do ultimately supports this master survival belief system.*

Almost all people have a controlling belief system like the "miserable" one mentioned above. People create unreasonable expectations so that they can judge themselves failures. People are overweight or in stressful situations, which create all kinds of diseases.

Why does a gambler expect to win? Logic says a gambler

will win as much as he loses. Most gamblers expect to win more than they lose. When logic sets in, they are miserable.

Who's happy? Only infants, until their own belief systems form and converge to smother their conscious enjoyment of life.

Why?

Man's life has not been easy. Evolution, survival of the fittest, slavery, torture, disease, plague, death, hell, famine, climate and financial depression have created misery for all.

There are no happy cultures. At anytime in the history of man, a child would have been able to observe parents and adults being miserable--and surviving. Mankind has endured misery and survived. *So the way to survive is to be miserable.*

When you are growing up, your instincts are alert constantly to finding out how to survive. In my case, I observed that the two most important people in my life were surviving, one by being angry and insecure, and the other by being insecure and worrying all the time.

This is not a total description of their personalities, but it was their basic survival roles. Since I wanted to survive, I inserted their negative views automatically, and unconsciously into my ego and my whole life operated out of it. All my belief systems had to conform to this master core belief system.

Even when we feel happy, there is that vague unexplainable fear as if we're waiting for the other shoe to drop. A pervasive overall feeling of impending doom. Expect to be miserable belief systems have been passed on from generation to generation. There appears to be no escape from this insertion. But, they can be discovered and eliminated.

"Ice Cream, Ice Cream, We All Scream for Ice Cream!"

Here is an example of a seemingly delightful belief system secretly conforming to <u>the master controlling belief system</u> and creating misery.

During therapy, I noticed that I ate a lot of ice cream. My whole family ate a lot of ice cream and it seemed natural to do so.

One of my most delightful childhood memories is of my father saying, "Ice cream, ice cream, we all scream for ice cream." My older sister would be dispatched to the store, while I waited with great anticipation. My mother divided the bulk ice cream under my close observation and unasked for supervision. I had to stand on a chair to provide this service, but I didn't mind. Those ice cream moments are the most happy of my entire childhood. There was no shouting or yelling, the family was content and at peace with itself, a rare calm moment.

The belief system formed was, "you can change any mood to peace, contentment, and happiness by eating ice cream." And it worked! And eating ice cream could also keep the good times rolling. The result was that whenever I was sad, lonely, depressed, upset, angry, or happy, I ate ice cream. Always vanilla and chocolate just like my family childhood memories. The amount I ate depended upon the situation. It took more ice cream to face a lonely weekend than a solitary lunch. There were one-pint situations, two-pint situations, and some took a half gallon.

The controlling belief system was difficult to locate, because it wasn't located in one tight place. It was everywhere.

The delightful change in my mood when I ate ice cream was a camouflage to create a depression which made me miserable which triggered my belief system to eat more ice cream.

For years I was unaware the sugar gave me a high and then a crash into sleep. I never connected the depression to the delightful eating of the ice cream. The ego used the ice cream to make me miserable by upsetting me about my will power and weight. Since ice cream changed my mood, I felt it was my friend.

If you look around in your life, you will find many similarities to my ice cream situation. Salt, sugar ,caffeine, fats, chocolate, and unreasonable goals are examples.

What would have been better was to not eat the ice cream in order to experience what came next. But I didn't. I ate the ice cream. The depression came, but did not reflect what was causing it.

I had been miserable all my life, depression was an old friend as far as I could remember. How was I to know? There wasn't anything to compare it with; How do you explain fire to a fish?

My constant companion of depression was the clue to a belief system that controlled my entire life and all my other belief systems. My root belief system was and to some small degree remains: "In order to survive, I have to be miserable." My ego began creating this for me from instructions inserted before I had developed my conscious memory. This early belief system's job is to keep me miserable so I can survive. All belief systems, when finally examined, trigger the root belief system.

Now that I know consciously that ice cream makes me miserable, and I have consciously decided I don't want to be miserable anymore, I am unable to eat ice cream without connecting it to the future misery it will create.

Belief systems do not allow this connection.

I now exist under a conscious concept that I am perfect the

way I am, regardless of my mood. If I want a mood change, I do what I call a "process" (See Chapter 20: Belief System Elimination Process, Page 217) on the mood I'm in to eliminate it. It works just the same as ice cream, but I don't end up being miserable. In fact, I get to feel great because I'm in control and the hero of my life!

Be the Hero of Your Life

We all have belief systems that make us miserable. We resist being helped because eliminating belief systems forces adjustments in our lives and takes effort. We know what it takes to attain every goal we desire, but we want it handed to us.

People actually choose misery rather than confronting the work necessary to be free and happy. It is safe and familiar to be miserable, and we are so used to it we hardly notice it anymore. The Ego agrees with you every time!

Ninety-nine percent plus of all the people alive today, if given a choice between being miserable and doing the work necessary to eliminate it, would accept the status quo. To accept the status quo is a belief system!

We have a choice about life. We do not have to experience it as being miserable. We can choose to experience it as joyful and happy.

Chapter 8

STRESS

Although the world is fifteen billion years old, the human race started to appear less than 100,000 years ago. Researchers say human beings have lived on earth about 800 lifetimes, many lasting fewer than 50 years. Most have been spent in caves.

How to survive and avoid death as a species was then and still is the game of life. Primitive man had a great way to determine what helped him to survive. When in danger of death, if primitive man acted and survived, he formed a belief system that said, "In order to survive, continue with the same behavior!"

If you faced death, felt hopeless and helpless to prevent it, but something happened that allowed you to survive, can you imagine what a high pitch your emotional and physical reactions would be as well as how deep the resulting belief insertion?

These belief systems formed on the fear of death level will be passed on forever because it involves survival of the species.

What were the life conditions of primitive man 100,000 years ago? He was starving, and when the opportunity to ease his starvation presented itself, he ate in a frenzy with gluttonous intensity constantly aware that at any moment a bigger beast could eat him and his food. A stressful situation to say the least! "In order to survive and prevent starvation, eat like a glutton" is the belief system formed.

Fear of death is the most powerful force in the human body. One hundred thousand years later, primitive man can still create

STRESS

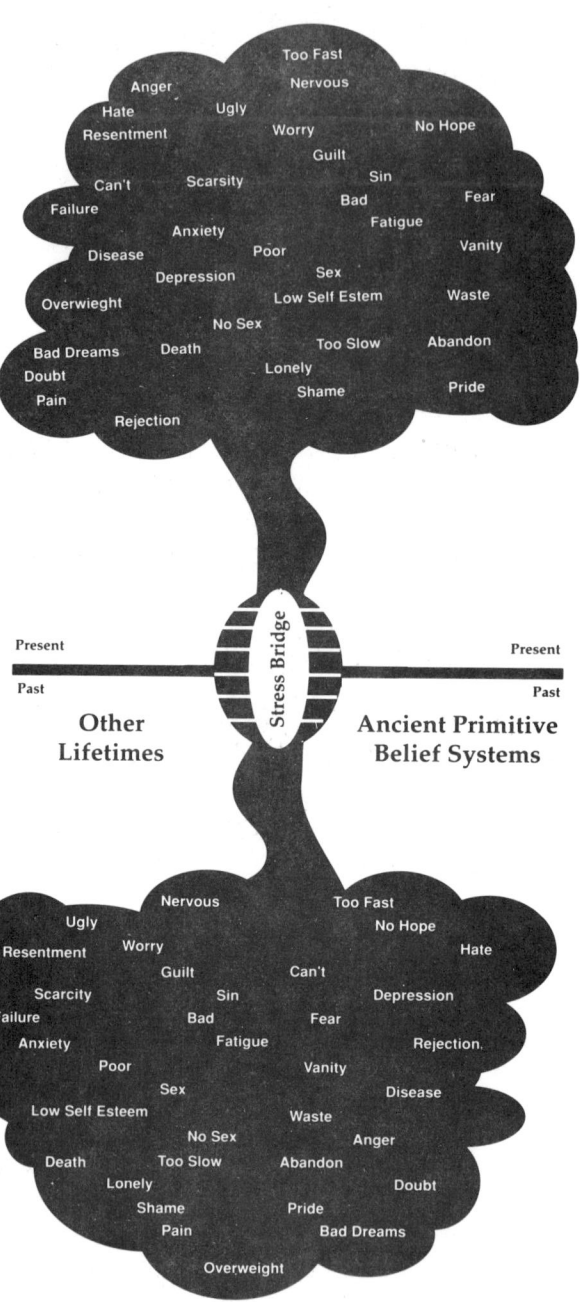

the emotions of fear of death in a modern body whenever a stressful incident creates similar, but not necessarily identical stress situations.

Belief systems are <u>not</u> subject to change according to each situation. If hunger pains meant starvation and death a hundred thousands years ago, they still mean the same thing today to the primitive person inside you.

These belief systems are quite basic and have to do with primitive survival. They deal with hiding from wild beasts in the woods: tearing a piece of meat from a dead animal with your teeth and swallowing it whole. Chewing took time that could be used to tear and swallow more before others ate what was left. How to find a cave, climb a tree, use a club and throw stones, plus other things that were useful a hundred thousand years ago.

Once your survival belief systems takes control, you are no different than a beast at a killing in the wild. The primitive belief system takes over creating violent reactions completely out of proportion to the present event. You eat so much because you fear dying of starvation.

When primitive man perceives there is no longer a danger of starvation, he will sink away leaving an over stuffed confused person.

The Common Ingredient is Stress

The common ingredient of every belief system back then and now, is stress. Stress is the bridge primitive man and his belief systems use to crossover into modern man. The absence of stress closes the door to him. Any current situation that creates stress creates opportunities for primitive man to act out prehistoric belief systems in order not to die.

How do we disconnect primitive man?

The belief system you have to eliminate is the one you created in this lifetime that causes the stress that lets primitive man cross over into your life.

Unconscious belief systems are formed at a very young age when a child has few experiences on which to draw upon to put the particular event in perspective.

In childhood, incidents happened that created stress, similar to but not totally identical to the fear of death. This triggered primitive man's awesome survival power. It is this power that makes the initial childhood belief system so deep and controlling. When you disconnect or eliminate this link, primitive man cannot cross over and control your behavior.

The result, if we lose consciousness, is that we have a primitive reaction to present day life. We get a survival reaction to a stressful, but not death threatening incident. The result often is unexplainable chaos.

Stress is universal in all men, past and present. It is predictable in that modern man in avoiding an accident will experience the same body changes as primitive man meeting a dangerous wild animal. Once the stress triggers the appropriate primitive belief system, the person will act it out to avoid death.

Our individual belief systems causes us to perceive stress situations differently. Each of us perceives crowds, noise, changes in location, fellow workers, family and friends, everyday hassles, doubt, and ambiguity differently.

Your belief system forces you into making an unconscious decision. You have no choice. If one understood this belief system, the person would be able to see it had nothing to do with will power.

What powerful force makes you stay overweight? If you

were a truck, would you drive around with an overload all the time?

We operate on this level every day. It is just a question of intensity as to what will trigger stress. We give up smoking and a crisis occurs creating stress; the stress activates a belief system that you must smoke or die. How can you not smoke? You feel you have no will power.

These belief systems may have made good sense 10,000 years ago, but not now.

Living With Near Death Intensity

Near death intensity of emotions sounds like a hard way to live, but we are living that way all the time, as horrible as it might sound.

As a result of living your life out of belief systems, you live at the level of survival. Primitive man perceived stress as lethal danger and the equal of a survival situation.

Every day the body lights up like a blinking neon sign. Stress on, stress off, stress on, stress off. Each time a belief system is triggered the body responds as if it is a death threat. Each experience of stress creates a heightened state of arousal. Literally, primitive man gets ready to fight or for flight.

Every gland is activated and secrets hormones. Extra sugar is pumped into the blood stream for extra energy. Eyes open wide. Our stomach stops working. All parts of the body tense up.

If primitive man enters our lives through stress and we are constantly under stress, we should be able to notice primitive behavior all around us. Lets take a look.

The alarm rings scaring a sleeping person (stress). A man is caught in a traffic jam and is late for work (stress). His expenses exceed his income (stress); his wife and children need dental work (stress); his job is overpowering him (stress). Sending his kids to college creates worry and anxiety about money (stress).

Other examples:

#1   An "all you can eat" restaurant is full of primitive people. They all arrived as modern people, but to get their money's worth (a stress inducer if there ever was one) they begin to eat like a bunch of beasts in the wild 100,000 years ago.

You sit down at the table and begin to eat like there is no tomorrow. Primitive man thinks it's his last meal. Why else would you be eating like a crazy man? Bingo, primitive belief systems take over and you get stuffed! Eating becomes survival. And, guess what happens?   Everybody leaves the restaurant bewildered, stuffed and unable to breathe feeling like throwing up and wanting ice cream at the same time.

They ate like they didn't know where their next meal was coming from.   Food was forced into their body against all common sense to avoid starving to death.   It was all a misunderstanding! Modern man was not starving, he just wasn't there!

The explanation is that primitive man inside us was awakened by stressful emotions and feelings and in order to survive, ate like a wild starving beast!

#2   Without food, primitive man will die. If you contemplate going on a diet and begin to concentrate on depriving yourself of food, primitive man will make you unconscious, and you will eat a great big snack.

When you are hungry, the intensity multiplies and you create stress similar to stress experienced by primitive man that triggers fear of starvation belief systems.

When you are hungry, stay conscious. Before you start to eat, ask yourself: "Are you starving to death? Do you have hunger pains? Who is eating the food, you or your primitive belief systems about food and survival?"

Not only don't eat, but use the time to realize you are not going to starve, and that you have triggered primitive starvation belief systems. Stay conscious and calm your primitive instincts.

#3   Accidently cut someone off while driving your car. You have threatened the other driver's life. Not really, but reality doesn't exist. The fright will trigger stress. The only reality is the driver's primitive man's reality and He will be screaming, yelling, and shaking his fists.

#4   An elevator full of strange people is stress just waiting to happen. Everybody looks down at the floor, or up at the floor indicator, but never into each other's eyes. People are too close for primitive man; there is no place to run.

Primitive man likes to have two alternatives in dangerous situations - fight or flight and one of them is not available. This creates stress.

#5   Who makes a late hit in football? (after the whistle) Is it primitive man or modern man? Who is in the boxing ring when both men are exhausted and still fighting?

#6   Consider a person making a speech.

The speaker who was relaxed and speaking casually, suddenly cannot breathe. His mouth and throat are dry. He stammers. His heart is racing. His palms are sweaty. His stomach knots. His hands and feet feel numb. Every muscle is tense.

The speaker saw a room full of friendly listeners; however, primitive man saw himself standing exposed in an open field with hundreds of hungry wild beasts, an incredibly dangerous situation. He takes control and prepares the body for fight or flight! The speech is a disaster.

#7   Stress is triggered when you are lost in a strange place. Primitive man wants to escape to his favorite tree or cave. He is exposed and vulnerable in a strange area.

#8   Silence will create stress instantly. Primitive man does not like silence. When he is walking through the forest nothing will cause him to come alert as will a sudden silence.

When you are in group conversation, people only half listen to what is being said, but let one person fail to respond as expected and the whole group will become alert.

#9   Here are some other examples:

1.   People who are conceited and get exposed or proven wrong = stress = a primitive belief system reaction.

2.   People who are too sensitive or vulnerable get their balloon pricked = stress = primitive belief system reaction.

3.   Insecure people--the cocky type--display bravado and run as if scared to death when confronted = stress = primitive belief system reaction.

4.   Any violent emotion like suspicion, greed, panic causes stress = primitive belief systems reaction.

5   Stage fright creates stress. Most people will not face a large group of people.

The Damage

Each of our bodies has an immune system which prevents diseases from entering our body. It works very well except when the body is under stress.

It can't handle the emotional discharges and hormonal changes of a near death experience and keep the body free from disease at the same time. The result is disease. The more the stress, the worse the disease. Stress creates disease which creates more stress.

Science has eliminated most deaths caused by infectious diseases. Stress related disease, like cancer, heart ailments, can be eliminated by removing belief systems that create survival reactions.

When primitive man experienced stress, he waited, and if he survived, he retreated to a safe place to recover. Total exhaustion created total relaxation. After a few hours the body returned to normal. Primitive man may have faced a life threatening incident once a month.

If you observe yourself, you will notice that primitive man fearing death keeps the body in a state of heightened arousal. It enters and leaves so fast the body cannot relax. Stress may happen to modern man 20 times a day. That doesn't leave a lot of recovery time.´

However, sometimes cancer or a heart attack creates an awareness or consciousness that shuts out primitive man. A person recovering from a heart attack or dying from cancer becomes very conscious. They notice the moment, and in relation to their imminent death, the things that used to upset them and create stress, seem meaningless and unimportant now.

So the cure, as always is awareness.

That's your job.   You do not have to live at the level of survival.

Primitive Man In Action

One of the most distinct memories I have is an amusement park event when I was less than four years old.   Although I have remembered it all these years, until recently, I did not realize that the belief systems created by this incident, controlled my whole relationships regarding females.

The incident is as follows:

My family and relatives were with me at the park.   Two of my male cousins and I were offered a ride on the "kitty cars."   There were one-seater fire trucks and two seater convertibles.   I wanted a convertible.   My two cousins each took a fire truck.

The only seat left was the back seat of a convertible as the front seat was already occupied by a little blond girl.   I wanted nothing to do with the back seat.   I wanted to drive and nothing could have been less attractive to me at that time than a girl!

(Little children tease and create horrible, painful and intense stress in each other.   Where do they learn this?   Of course, parents say things that create belief systems without knowing it.   Obviously, I had one about girls and I was not yet four.)

I was put in the back seat of the convertible.   I was helpless to prevent this, because it happened so fast.   The ride started before I could even cry or protest to my parents.   My fantasy and ambition was to drive the car, not to sit in the back.   Then I realized there was a girl in the front and she was driving.

I blushed beat red which caused the people I depended on for love and approval the most to laugh at me.   I became violently upset, feeling helpless, angry, totally humiliated and ashamed to be in the back of a car that a girl was driving. At the time I would have preferred death, to what I was living through.

What you have here is a body excited and experiencing stress similar to what primitive man would have experienced in a near death experience. The result is that I created a belief system with the emotional power of fear of death. This belief system was written on the soft slate of a child before the age of reason who had no way to integrate it.

Unfortunately, I created a belief system from the experience that said: "In order to survive you have to create situations where woman will make you feel humiliated, ashamed, upset, helpless, and angry." This belief system controlled my behavior for fifty years.

Anytime I had a relationship with a woman, this belief system activated, and I was unconscious of my feelings and behavior. For decades, a woman would trigger uncomfortable feelings in me at the deepest levels, similar to what I experienced in the kitty-car, and similar to feelings experienced by primitive man when in danger of death. How frustrating for me and anyone trying to have a relationship with me.

The incident did <u>not</u> really have life-threatening ingredients. However, primitive man cannot make distinctions. He recognized similar feelings and emotions, and activated primitive reactions. What was supposed to be a wonderful time at an amusement park created a belief system nightmare for me. There was no real danger, but I perceived danger and primitive man did the rest.

We all have similar experiences and belief systems and they too were written with survival power on your slate and you are placed into primitive automatic behaviors on a daily basis too!

When you live at the level of survival, the same reaction will be triggered 10,000 times in a row! Without going back and reexperiencing the initial event, the same reaction will repeat itself forever.

By eliminating this kitty car belief system, I was able to eliminate much of the grief I had carried with me about girls. Without eliminating this belief system, I would still be doomed to unconscious automatic behaviors regarding women.

WHO DO YOU KNOW AND LOVE THAT WOULD BENEFIT IF YOU LOANED THEM THIS BOOK?

1. _____

2. _____

3. _____

4. _____

5. _____

6. _____

7. _____

8. _____

9. _____

10. _____

Chapter 9

CREATING BELIEF SYSTEMS IS BIG BUSINESS

Whatever business you are in, you know that the key to profits is repeat business. Repeat business comes about when people buy your product out of habit and no longer think about it. People buy the same car visit the same stores and buy the same things over and over each week.

The way to create a consistent purchasing habit regarding your product is to get a customer to self-insert a favorable belief system about your product.

Once this belief system is inserted it can be passed on to children and future generations. So owners of businesses are willing to spend huge amounts of money to insert belief systems that cause repeat purchases of their product.

Your brain and your children's brain are constantly being bombarded by vendors and power seekers attempting to insert belief systems, using unconscious means. Here is an example:

Baby powder has a heavy sweet smell to it. Babies form a belief system that associates that smell with purity, fresh, clean, safe, and secure; because all those things happen to a baby when baby powder is being used. Advertisers know this.

So if you want to sell a product that will make people think they feel fresh, clean, or secure make it smell like baby powder. The smell will actuate the belief systems. Reality will disappear replaced by the belief system memory of safe, secure, clean, and fresh and an automatic, unconscious purchase will take place.

If you want your boyfriend to feel safe, secure, fresh, and clean about you, ask his mother what type of baby powder she used and match the perfume in the baby powder with your deodorant. You can't miss! Not only smell, but all the senses are used this way by advertisers to make you unconsciously do what they want.

Advertisers on Saturday morning are creating belief systems in your children that will last for generations. Almost everyone shops in the same grocery store every week. The grocery owner will do all in his power not to make you aware of your blind habit. You will do all in your power not to wake up because change creates unfamiliarity which creates painful anxiety.

All leaders of nations have branches of government specifically created using television, radio, and newspapers to attempt to get the population to self-insert favorable belief systems about their government, and they are very successful.

No where is this craft more perfected than in the church business. People remain in the same religion for centuries. Whole nations identify with their religion. What child ever gets a chance to choose his or her religion? Indeed, what child is conscious of a choice existing?

Consider for example:

When I was in grammar school there were signs on the school walls that said to be healthy, I should smoke Camels and eat the following foods daily:

      Meat Group - two or more servings;
      Milk Group - three or more servings;
      Vegetables and Fruits - four of more servings;
      Bread and Cereals - four or more servings.

Remember "MORE DOCTORS SMOKE CAMELS THAN ANY OTHER

CIGARETTE."

Whose signs are these? The signs were given to the schools by the companies selling these products. The schools provided the wall space.

The executives in these industries are interested in inserting belief systems that will promote the use of their products, so that the stockholders will be happy.

We are the stockholders. We permit it all because we have belief systems that we need never ending money.

If you want to be rich, figure out how to advertise to children before they reach the age of reason. Major corporations will break down your door to throw money at you.

As a result of allergies, I have developed polyps that clog my nostrils. Each allergy attack closes my nose down completely. I should avoid caffeine, sugar, dairy products, and alcohol as they tend to create mucus in my nose. As a kid, my life was one big sinus headache.

These products are still heavily advertised.

Who is Protecting the Child, Where are the Parents?

Where are the free signs on the school walls telling the little children how lethal some of the above items are ? No profit-No signs!

NOW YOU KNOW WHY YOU TOLERATE POLLUTED AIR AND WATER, DRINK AND EAT POISONS AND ACCEPT ILL HEALTH AND EARLY DEATH. BECAUSE YOU ARE YOUR BELIEF SYSTEMS.

Get the facts. If not for your sake, do it for your children! They are being programmed everyday just as you were. Just watch 30 minutes of television Saturday morning for proof.

The next time your child cries hysterically for a toy, you will know what stimulated such a response.

WHAT PARENTS DO YOU KNOW THAT WOULD BENEFIT FROM READING THIS BOOK?

WOULD YOUR CHILDREN, CO-WORKERS, FRIENDS ENJOY READING THIS BOOK? YOUR BROTHER, SISTER?

Chapter 10

ALL BUT PERSONAL AUTHORITY IS INSANITY

The function of authority is to maintain the status quo.

Authority is a unconscious, gigantic, automatic, collective belief system inserted deep and early in our lives and seldom questioned. We obey our parents and everybody they obey. We do not question authority in government, corporations, schools or society. We invest our whole life in the authority of the status quo.

The Status Quo

Our ego is our belief systems. The total of our egos is called the collective belief system. The collective belief system is the status quo.

Who guards our status quo? <u>We do</u>! We are ready to war and die to protect it. We have a belief system that says, "If we invalidate our belief systems, we invalidate ourselves."

All powers desire and promote the status quo belief systems until it becomes the accepted wisdom. Belief systems create obedience! Authorities create belief systems to control entire nations.

Our belief systems are what we agree is our sanity.

Leaders in a society or government reflect its people. Our leaders are about to blow up the world; they are ruining the environment, and conducting suicidal wars. If they succeed, will the history of the universe judge the earth as having been insane?

In an insane world, a sane person would be committed, or be forced to become insane to be judged normal. If suicide is insanity, what does it say about <u>our</u> status quo?

How Does The Status Quo Program A Child Forever?

Status quo belief systems have been around for centuries and determine what is normal behavior and what will be passed on.

A child must conform to appear normal. A child that does not appear normal is sent for counseling. If the child belief systems are not the same as the status quo, the psychiatrist will likely judge the child insane.

The status quo uses death, hell, loss of paradise, loss of love, inculcated fears, threats, symbols, monsters, rituals, colors, smells, fairy tales, children stories, and every diabolical, painful, emotional, and social humiliation conceivable to mutilate a child's mind until they think and see the world as we, the status quo, see it.

Status Quo Objections

When the top says an idea won't work, it doesn't mean it won't work as much as it means that the idea is upsetting a present "status quo" belief system. <u>The greater the upset, the more established the belief system is that you are trying to change and the greater the opposition will be to it.</u>

For instance:

If you were an electric company, would you be interested in solar power? Not unless you discovered a way to put a meter on the sun. The meter would prolong the status quo of you being in control.

To Change the Top, Change the Bottom

Authority is a collective belief system. To change the top, you first have to change the bottom. Unless we change, they cannot! When you change the individual level, all the rest has to change since they reflect us in total.

If you remove your belief system about authority, then to a degree, you will be weakening the collective belief system. Having the ability to change yourself to a better person will have a more powerful effect on the world than all authority combined. You can destroy power by removing your inserted belief systems.

Status Quo and Concrete

We all have a big investment in social customs.

The Pilgrims ate turkey on Thanksgiving because it was there and the price was right--free! Why do you eat it? Because eating turkey on Thanksgiving is an inserted belief system passed on from generation to generation.

The South's status quo belief systems about slavery caused a bloody civil war. A whole way of life was threatened.

Additional belief systems are inserted giving glorious honors and prizes to heroes for not questioning the status quo. (History is written by the victorious.)

If we have a belief system about everything, then our destiny is set in concrete. Little opportunity exist for individual spontaneity and self-exploration. How can we change our destiny if individuals and nations operate blindly out of unconscious belief systems.

Politics and Computer Chips

You have to be numb and blind to practice politics. Without

a set of deeply inserted belief systems, that say power is survival, what person could endure the personal attacks, contradictory positions, broken promises, feelings of humiliation, etc. to get elected?

The chip will change everything. People will have power and direct their leaders in precisely what they want. (But only if they're conscious!) Accurate information will be abundant and opposing views available. Politicians will get instant voting returns from telephone and television to guide them. This computer power will be directly accessible by people for all purposes.

Chapter 11

RELIGION

A religion is a group of belief systems about God created by man to answer all unanswered questions.

Since the beginning of time, primitive societies lived in fear. There were no answers for thunder, lightning, storms, comets, and most of all, death. Not having an answer creates anxiety.

Man created belief systems about God to answer fearful questions and relieve anxiety. When we are anxious and scared we turn to authority for assurance and direction, and will believe anything. People motivated by power know this.

Now, suppose you are authority and you want people to obey you and do a specific job. However, people want to do what they want to do. You can conquer them through force and make them slaves, but you need guards. Who watches the guards? More guards? It gets expensive and doesn't work. How to get the job done without costly guards was the problem.

Suppose we could get people to self-insert a belief system in which they will accept as truth, without question, whatever we say or tell them. Suppose further that we can ignite that belief system at will whenever we want a specific job done.

"Eureka" said the people wanting power. Create an all-knowing, all-powerful God who can be everywhere, see everything, keep track of everything, even when no one is within fifty miles.

Create "GOD" as the answer to all unanswered questions.

Create dogma and the desired rules. Say God wants these rules obeyed. Create eternal hell as the punishment for not obeying.

Create sin, self-doubt, self-hate, guilt, and insecurity with periodic self-confession; and there is no escape. Then, create a belief system that says, all the previous inserted belief systems are valid and should never be examined or questioned.

Over generations, it becomes the custom to accept the unfounded dogma as fact and the word of God. When properly done, each human will automatically pass the entire belief system on to their children and their children's children forever. Does this sound familiar?

So the answer was self-enforcement created by belief systems about God.

We go to church to be monitored, receive new and updated belief systems, and to put money in the collection box.

Confession is a great tool of church leaders to constantly remind us how bad and imperfect we are. Why are we taught to confess our sins and faults and not our virtues?

So we will feel badly about ourselves and since we got this way by self-thought, we will stop thinking and obey them. They will tell us what GOD wants done.

Going Within

No religion will deny we yearn to be spiritual or that the most direct route to God is by going within. Your heart knows more about going within than all the religions combined!

When we worship the religion, we can't reach God because religious belief systems are a barrier to knowing God. These belief systems tell us to have faith and not trust our feelings and inner urges.

Religious belief inculcation (drilling) starts before memory so beliefs inserted at that time are untouchable through any recollection. St. Dominic said, "Give me a child before he is six, and I will make him a Catholic the rest of his life." Belief systems are insertions never questioned or remembered at this age. It's put there before it can be judged.

Religion is a beehive of belief systems. A child given a religion will likely remain within that religion forever. Giving a kid a religion before the age of reason is like having part of his brain cut away. By having a religion, so many belief systems are added to the psyche it takes forever to pierce them.

Look around you. Why are Jewish, Catholic, and Protestant children practicing the same religion as their parents? They don't drive the same cars or wear the same type of clothes.

We laugh at other people's religious customs and beliefs, but we never question our own. It's like someone programming your computer at the factory before it's shipped to you. You'll never know what buttons have been pushed, so you will not be able to deprogram it. **This is not funny.** We are talking about the brain you are presently using to try to make sense out of this world you live in.

If I were the Devil, I would invent religion to control the masses. Once you get religion going, love is impossible. Religious wars create havoc and mayhem to this day and not a single person can produce God, or has ever met God.

Belief systems about God are strong, violent and unfriendly. If you want to play a dangerous sport someday, ask a person to justify some absolute belief they have about their religion.

At present, most of us see the Middle East as an unsolvable

muddle of religious belief systems.

Normal people negotiate a settlement based on logic. For example, if ten identical parts are to be divided, each party will receive five. If the parts cannot be divided equally, an independent entity establishes "value" and the difference might be handled with money.

But when religious fanatics negotiate, they say: "Give me all ten parts, or I will blow up the world." Their logic is based on Divine Right which is a belief system inserted early and is virtually untouchable. The ego creates a covering belief system that states the first belief system is valid, doesn't have to be verified, or ever examined. Thus, they will reject any imaginable compromise. This is why religious zealots appear to be crazy. There are two solutions to this problem. Eliminate the belief system or eliminate the people who have the belief system.

Biology

In biology, every species does what is needed by whatever means, to reproduce itself.

With religion, the key is to insert your belief system first into the unprotected brain. Domination using broken promises, perfidy, and betrayal are the most effective.

A missionary is an example of a human being up to his eyeballs with belief systems. Missionaries have destroyed entire cultures.

American Indians confined to reservations starving and suffering smallpox from infested blankets and not knowing why or how it happened are easily convinced to join a new religion if it means health and food.

The healthy missionaries appear to have a better God and

the conversion takes place. The missionaries were given exclusive right to certain Indians reservations by the government so some are Methodist, some Catholic, etc., and will be for centuries if not forever.

The Philippine Islands are Catholic because the Jesuits got there first. The Crusades were a holy war about different belief systems. So was the Inquisition and the Holocaust!

You were not born with a belief system about God. If you were not born with it, then it's a belief system. It means you are unconscious concerning decisions about God.

Choices

There are lots of religions to choose if you desire such a choice. And, if you are afraid, you will surely choose. Many of them sound pretty good to me. Are you worried about death? How about heaven? Reincarnation?

"Do what I say, accept my answers, or go to hell," covers a lot of the dogma.

We have been given incredible information about before life, and after life, but no proof. Why don't we seek proof? Because we have a belief system that says, "Don't look, just believe!

Karma had to have been invented by the powers who were in charge. If I'm rich, and a powerful mob of people are poor, what better answer to tell them that their miserable existence is not your fault, but theirs, a direct result of their evil past lives.

The only way to avoid another miserable life in the future is to continue to live a miserable life now, and let me enjoy my luxuries and riches. Neat as four fingers of scotch.

Karma is our belief systems in action. It's a path of life with the least resistance. Do nothing and consciousness will be buried by belief systems. Taking responsibility for your life is the opposite of Karma.

You can be the victim, or the hero, of your life. Karma is being the victim. Discovering, and eliminating belief systems is being the hero. You can tell the future with Karma. The rest of your life will be similar to what is true for you now, only more and more belief systems will be added to continually reduce vitality.

Of all the philosophies, I like Zen the most. You ask the Zen master a question and he hits you with a stick and sends you away to look at a blank wall for two months. After he hits you with a stick enough times, and you're sick and tired of looking at blank walls, it dawns on you that the answer is within and asking anyone, including the Zen master, for ultimate answers is absurd.

Zen gives it to you straight. Stop looking for answers in other structures and people. It is not there. You have the answer within yourself. No proof here, but at least you are given responsibility for your life.

How about Taoism, Confucianism, Buddhism, Hinduism, or the other Eastern religions or creeds? Lots of answers, but no proof.

Then there is the, "No God Gang." These belief systems are opposite from the God Gang.

My religion is that life is a poker game. In order to play, you have to accept the original cards. (i.e. Belief Systems) After that, you can keep playing and eliminating the cards until you are totally conscious. (you are One with God)

What's Right?

We hold belief systems that say religious zealot's belief

systems are wrong. What is right? (What is right and wrong based on a belief system has little chance of being the same.)

THE ONLY CHANCE OF A SOLUTION IS THE ELIMINATION OF BELIEF SYSTEMS IN ALL PEOPLE. THEN ALL RELIGION WILL BE CONSCIOUS ENOUGH TO TRULY KNOW GOD.

One of my fantasies is that there exists in Africa a huge ant hill, and the ants have the same set of belief systems as we do. There are ant philosophers, ant Buddhists, ant scientists, as well as Catholic, Protestant, and Jewish ants. They too, using belief systems, have almost relieved fear and anxiety just like us. Then one day, a farmer bulldozes the ant hill and plants beans.

Surrendering to an ISM

The belief systems of Jews, Catholics, Protestants, Baptists, Black, Red, Yellow, Brown, and White people, are what separates us and makes us feel exclusive. All ISM's are belief systems and do the same thing: Hinduism, Moslemism, Capitalism, Communism.

Belief System Expectations And Failures

When we are setting our goals and expectations, we choose the most successful people with perfect intellect and taste as our models. Our parents help by giving us their past and an unattainable model. We also absorb unreasonable goals unconsciously from our observations of T.V. and advertisements. If we fail to achieve these goals, we suffer self-contempt and revulsion and <u>judge</u> ourselves a failure.

And, we all fail to live up to our expectations. Who does not feel bored, guilty, a sinner, a misfit, an outcast, impotent in some situations?

Even when we succeed, our self-doubt brings us down because our belief systems are unreasonable, unattainable, and ridiculous. Yet we do not change the belief system. We seek relief by avoiding responsibility for ourselves. We give ourselves over to a cause, a religion, alcoholism, revolution. What have you?

A belief system passed down over the ages by unconscious observation is: "Blame what ails you on something external (church, government, etc.)." This belief system is observable in all people but ourselves. The key rules are: (1) deny self-blame by blaming something else; (2) make the something else something you have no control over.

We hope to avoid the pain of failing to live up to our extravagant belief system about success by exchanging our freedom of choice to follow the elegant and unproven promises of an "ism". We say we believe, for only by believing can we avoid the pain and responsibility for our failure.

We infect ourselves with this failure malady and falsely believe losing ourself in a collective whole (ISM) will cure us. What we lose is our individual distinctiveness and ability to control our destiny. We give up our judgment and our free will.

The pain of personal responsibility for failure goes away; and we become a "nobody" within a group of nobodies and become like bakery dough to be kneaded into any form the "ISM" desires. You are free from freedom, incomplete and insecure forever.

We join an ISM where the hard decisions are made by some vague and remote authority. The more remote, the better. The perfect "remote" is one that can't be verified nor rewarded nor understood in our lifetime, but all responsibilities can be surrendered to it.

Surrender

It feels good to give up choice "to turn your life over to an,"ISM". Yet who is responsible if the ISM fails to fulfill our expectations? And how do you get to know what the Ism wants? Who tells you? Who created the Ism? Did they have belief systems? Are you operating unconsciously out of their belief systems by way of the Ism?

Our revulsion and self-contempt for ourselves are belief systems. We are born free and choose not to be. We scrap our freedom to avoid responsibility.

Chapter 12

CRISIS AS AN OPPORTUNITY

A crisis seems like a loss of control; but it is an opportunity to seize your life from your ego and assert your identity.

A crisis is a golden opportunity to observe the belief systems that control you. These belief systems created this crisis. If you want to avoid a similar crisis or shorten the one you are in, eliminate the belief systems.

A crisis is a breakdown, not of the person, but of the person's belief systems. It happens when the event is bigger than the belief system the ego created to contain it. The belief system is unable to shield reality from penetrating the consciousness of the person. Examples of crisis are death of a loved one, divorce, moving, losing job, or retiring.

The crisis creates violent mental, physical, and emotional upheavals in the body. The Ego searches for past similar conditions and dredges up every crisis you ever had in any area of your whole life all at once!

The result is that many core belief systems cannot be contained. Every bad experience belief system you ever had surfaces and overwhelms you. You feel helpless, hopeless, powerless, painfully unloved, isolated, deserted, frightened, naked in facing your anxiety, fears, depression, rejection, and anger.

This creates unbearable stress and activates primitive man's fear of death causing an awesome assault on the mortal, physical, and emotional body.

Seize the moment!

While you're upset and excited, do a process. (See Chapter 20: Belief System Elimination Process, Page 217). Do it right in the middle of the upset and the source of the original belief system will surface. Write it down in full detail. Everything you can remember: feelings, thoughts, smells, everything.

Do a Process!

The more processes you do at this time, the more core belief systems you will reveal, eliminate, or weaken and the next crisis will not be as bad because there will be fewer belief systems to attack you.

In some cases, you will experience many deep breaths, memories, and past events and still feel overwhelmed. Keep doing it. Stay conscious and keep acknowledging your physical and emotional feelings. These core belief systems combinations have been growing for years and possibly centuries.

It may take weeks of continual processes to wear away the compacted combinations formed over time. Deep breaths are the proof that something is happening.

Because I did not understand the extent of the density of the compacted belief systems it took twenty years to eliminate smoking and ice cream belief systems.

I kept giving up because nothing seemed to be happening. I felt I wasn't succeeding when actually I was wearing away a gigantic accumulation. One day it disappeared.

You do not have to understand what belief system is being eliminated or how. Nobody understands how the ego accumulates or eliminates belief systems. Trying to figure it out will only limit your progress. If it is eliminated, rejoice!

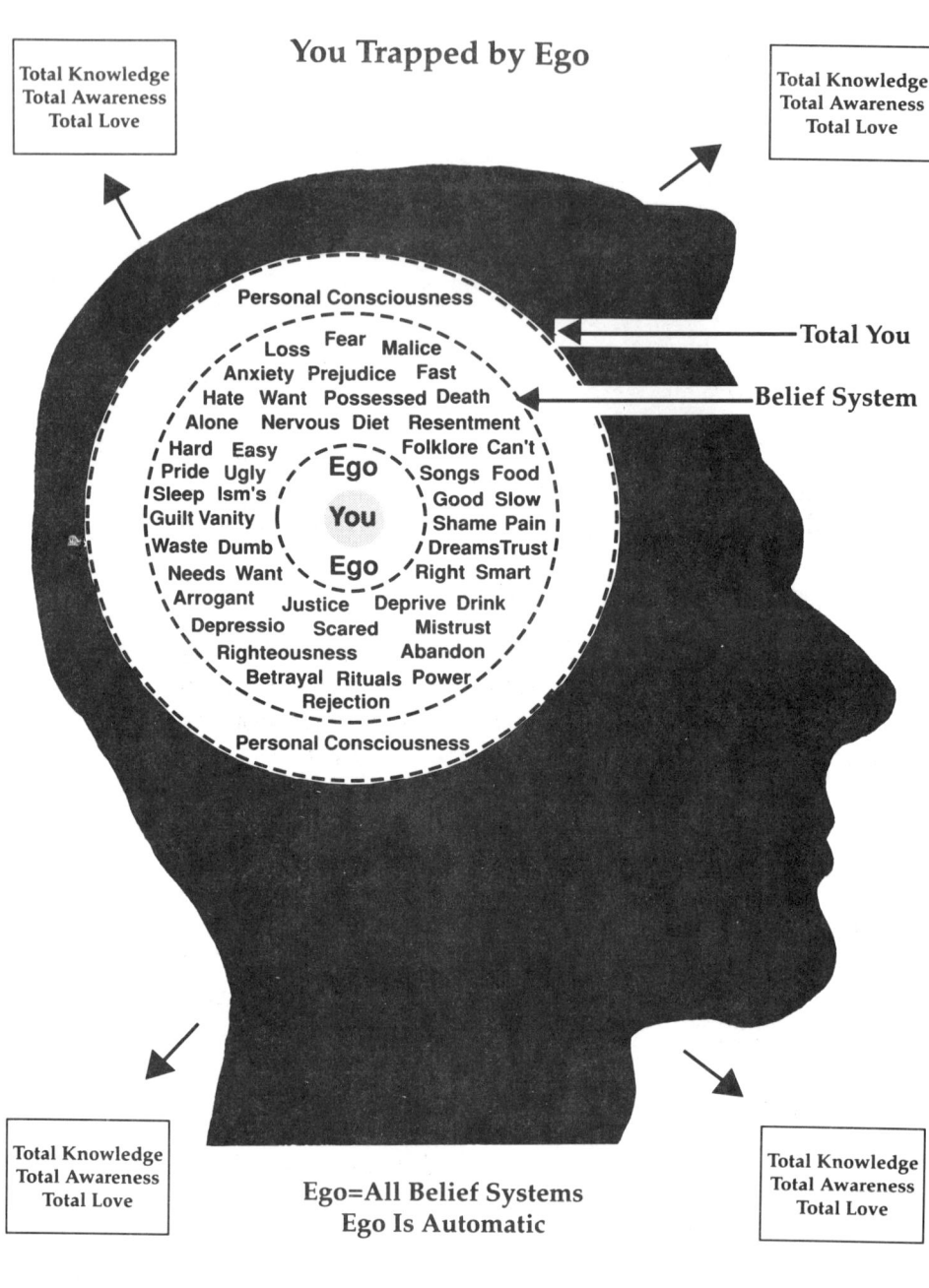

You Trapped by Ego

Total Knowledge
Total Awareness
Total Love

Total Knowledge
Total Awareness
Total Love

Personal Consciousness

Loss Fear Malice
Anxiety Prejudice Fast
Hate Want Possessed Death
Alone Nervous Diet Resentment
Hard Easy Folklore Can't
Pride Ugly **Ego** Songs Food
Sleep Ism's Good Slow
Guilt Vanity **You** Shame Pain
Waste Dumb **Ego** DreamsTrust
Needs Want Right Smart
Arrogant Justice Deprive Drink
Depressio Scared Mistrust
Righteousness Abandon
Betrayal Rituals Power
Rejection

Personal Consciousness

Total You

Belief System

Total Knowledge
Total Awareness
Total Love

Total Knowledge
Total Awareness
Total Love

Ego=All Belief Systems
Ego Is Automatic

Chapter 13

EGO

Your ego is the sum total of all your belief systems, good or bad, small or large. When you are unconscious, you are your belief systems completely.

The ego is a mindless executor of your belief systems. It does not fear good, constructive, positive belief systems. What it fears is no belief systems; because then it would not exist. Right now it follows whatever willy-nilly belief systems our observations create, and in its dark genius tries to make sense out of all of it.

If you were an ego and you knew that you were one hundred percent your belief systems, you would do all in your power to prevent any of them from disappearing. The ego creates belief systems to rule you and to ensure its survival. If the ego succeeds, you will feel and think that you are your belief systems and nothing else. Thus, your ego will survive as long as you do.

The ego considers itself separate and unique from nature and God and voluntarily will not let itself die.. The ego considers the loss of a belief system as a partial death and consequently, suffers perpetual anxiety about death. Anxiety is a product of the ego, not of being. The reality is that eliminating belief systems creates the birth of the pure self.

The ego operates in the past and future, but not the present. When something happens to a person in the present, it immediately compares it to a similar event (belief system) in the past and creates the past behavior for the present event.

In this way, the ego creates future behavior from past behavior. Except for flashes of consciousness that slip through (which are responsible for all progress), we are still drones. The same thing that happened to the dog happened to our consciousness.

Danger!

Furthermore, if you succeed in eliminating a belief system, you will be less miserable, therefore have less incentive or desire to eliminate another one. However, this elimination will threaten the ego. The ego will seize this opportunity to convince you to stop. Be on your guard.

The deeper you go, the more the ego will resist. And the ego is very powerful. Try to give up a lifetime habit like smoking, drinking, or overeating; and you'll see what I'm talking about.

This book has been very difficult to write. Is it possible that the collective ego is hampering me?

Pure Consciousness

GRIEF

ANGER

VAGUE CONTROLLING
BELIEF SYSTEM OCEAN

GUILT

ANXIETY

REJECTION

Chapter 14

VAGUE CONTROLLING BELIEF SYSTEMS

Imagine an ocean where all the water is actually vague belief systems. In the ocean there are upsets islands called anger, grief, and anxiety. You are a ship and the only time you are conscious is when you are out of the water and not on an island, in the air!

These vague controlling belief systems are formed by a combination of events that we experienced and survived. The ego in its dark genius combines these random events to form a group of rules that are used to keep us unconscious of our behavior until a major upset occurs.

Except for major upsets, we operate most of the time out of vague controlling belief systems. Vague controlling belief systems come and go, but they are always there waiting to fill in the conscious gaps between major upsets.

Vague controlling belief systems are what you wake up to in the morning when you don't feel right but there aren't any major upsets; a general feeling of impending doom, worldly gloom. We eat, smoke, drink, watch tv, make telephone calls, and attend movies to bury them.

On a busy day, major upset reactions make vague controlling belief systems unnoticeable but at moments of isolated quiet, (nighttime, early morning, lonely weekends) unconscious emotions, feelings, and attitudes emerge that trigger undefinable, indescribable moods without a source.

It is hard to describe how you feel emotionally or physically. However, anyone who has even been in an uncomfortable mood, bored or depressed will need no more explanation.

Sometimes I feel my body needs a can of oil. How do you convey that? If you feel indescribable, you are dealing with a "vague controlling" belief system.

What percentage of your total life can you remember? Where is the rest? We don't remember because we were made unconscious most of the time by vague controlling belief systems and the rest of the time by major upset belief systems. What we do remember were created by flashes of consciousness.

You can switch or operate out of 30-50 all encompassing, conflicting, combining, overlapping, or interchanging controlling belief systems at the same time. Like a thousand snakes in a pit.

For instance:

I'll be happy when "X" happens.
It's me against the world.
I'm not good enough!
Another day, another dollar.
When do I get a break?
When will it ever end?
Same old routine. I'm getting nowhere.
Oh, God, I'm bored.
Oh, God, I'm stuck.
Life is ugly, there is no hope.
Society is out to get me.
I will always be poor, lonely, depressed.
Live is empty and then you die.
Can't beat the system.
Hard to define overall feeling of black.
In a "downer" for no reason.
Don't feel right but you can't put your finger on it.

No matter how hard I try, I'll always fail.
I'm unlovable.
Whatever I do, it won't work.
Other people (they) are in control.
I'm hopeless, helpless, powerless.
I have no control over my fate.
Weary, and I feel terrible.
I'm doomed.
I'm always wrong. Don't be wrong. Don't admit your wrong.
Go for the money!
Something good will happen.
Play it safe.
I chose the wrong life.
I'm exhausted

I'm Not Good Enough

Every person that ever existed since the beginning of time felt this way . From the day you are born you feel overwhelmed by circumstances that make you feel you are not good enough.

Logically, if none of us are good enough then we must be all equal. If we are all equal then we are all good enough!

Unfortunately, we individually created our belief systems and individually have to discover and eliminate them.

Go for the Money

We look to our parents and people we respect to give us guidance during our formative years. Most information and advice will say: "GO FOR THE MONEY!" Be a doctor or a lawyer or a broker. The inserted belief system is: "To be happy and successful with peace of mind you must acquire money." Following a life that merely satisfies someone else's expectation lacks vitality and can never be fully rewarding.

I Chose the Wrong Life

Everyone of us in a quiet moment wonders if another way of life would be better. It's an undefined vague feeling. Perhaps, because you want it so much and it's so unattainable, just thinking about it is too painful.

How come since we really knew what we wanted, we didn't get it? What happened is that we followed a belief system.

It is better to follow your interests and pursue what you like to do. It will not seem like work so you will not mind the many hours you have to put in to be successful. Being successful will have less meaning if you like the work you do.

People who are unbelievably successful continue to work because they love what they do. They always wanted to do it. Their success just makes them more able to do what they enjoy doing. When you follow a belief system work is never-ending and unrelieved. Your happiness always seems in the future.

The message of God is, if you want divine power, follow your heart, do what gives you conscious joy. You can't take your money with you, but you can enjoy everyday by doing work you like that gives you a feeling of accomplishment. You will experience aliveness and creativity. Yesterday was great, today is wonderful and tomorrow better still.

Me Against the World

We are born and forever face opposition from the world or so it seems. Actually the world is just there, but it appears to be fighting us. We need food, shelter and other comforts and it appears to not want to give them to us. We experience this and survive. Therefore to survive we have to be against the world. The result is conflict and confusion instead of cooperation.

Play it Safe

Playing it safe is what we mostly do because we were hurt when we did not and survived. It is a tremendous act of courage to overcome groups of childhood belief systems, plus all the play it safe advice from your parents. We are told all our lives to deprecate ourselves so most of our belief systems are negative about risk taking. With belief systems like this, its a tremendous effort to take a risk. You have to keep trying and taking risks to love yourself. When you don't play it safe and succeed tremendous conscious joy of your basic uniqueness occurs.

I'll be Happy When "X" Happens

People who have a controlling belief system not to be happy until "X" happens, will continually change "X" so it doesn't ever happen. Their controlling belief system is: In order to survive, I must be unhappy. For example:

> I'll be happy when I'm in nursery school.
> I'll be happy when I'm in first grade.
> I'll be happy when I'm in secondary school.
> I'll be happy when I'm in college.
> I'll be happy when I'm in the outside world.
> I'll be happy when I'm in married.
> I'll be happy when I have children.
> I'll be happy when I'm more successful.
> I'll be happy when I have a bigger house.
> I'll be happy when I retire.
> I'll be happy when my heart is stronger.
> I'll be happy if I had all my teeth.
> I'll be happy if sex was better.
> I'll be happy if my eyesight was better.
> I'll be happy if my digestion improves.
> I'll be happy when the pain stops.
> I'll be happy when I die.

Being unhappy can be accomplished in many ways. Once you understand how the game is played, you can see how you are setting up your own misery.

Eliminate belief systems that set standards that are impossible to achieve. or compare you with others. Evaluate yourself only against yourself. You don't know what advantages or disadvantages other people have, so forget it. Are you better today than you were yesterday? A month ago? A year ago? Success is relative only to you.

Remove the belief system and decide to be happy. Living and being happy is a function of deciding to be that way. It has nothing to do with anything else, money, friends, love, etc. People who decide to be happy, will be, regardless of the circumstances. So decide right now to be happy.

Happiness, Energy, Anything You Want Is A Thought Away

You come home after 12 hours hard work, you're exhausted; you can hardly lift your finger. All you can think of is getting to bed and sleeping forever. The phone rings and Mr./Ms. Wonderful wants to have dinner, is it possible? Yes, of course it is! You are alive and full of energy and stay that way the whole evening.

An idea in the middle of the night can wake you from a dead sleep bright as the sun and you will work for 48 hours without getting tired. Where did the energy come from? It was there all the time. However, you were operating out of a vague controlling belief system that says you should be exhausted if you work hard for twelve hours, so you were.

Mr./Ms. Wonderful shifted you from one controlling belief system to another. The second belief system said you should be full of energy and joy, so you were.

In the above case, you were operating and switching

controlling belief systems unconsciously, but it's just as easy to change them consciously. If you wake up in the morning in an unwanted mood, do a process (See Chapter 20: Belief System Elimination Process, Page 217), merge with your innerself and eliminate the belief system. If the next mood doesn't satisfy you, do it again. Over time, you will eliminate all your unwanted bad morning moods and start waking up feeling wonderful and full of vitality!

Your mood right now is a result of your present belief system. If you do not like the mood you are in, merge and see what comes up.

Any mood that comes up anywhere is an opportunity to discover a belief system. Something triggered the mood. What was it? The elimination of the belief system will move you to another place which is another opportunity. (See Chapter 12: Crisis as an Opportunity, Page 111)

Consciousness is slipping through the cracks all the time; but we do not recognize it. Pay attention! Watch for the deep breath.

Chapter 15

MAJOR UPSET BELIEF SYSTEMS

A. OVEREATING

Belief Systems and Normal Weight

Eating is an area where the most complicated, densely compacted, deeply hidden belief systems are found. Primitive man's power base is here. By the time you solve your eating problems, you will have eliminated all your belief systems to a large degree. Giving up smoking is relatively easy compared to eating because eating belief systems start at birth.

A tremendous amount of hunger belief systems have nothing to do with being hungry. Childhood belief systems inserted before memory create automatic behavior. Eating was survival at first.

You unconsciously created many belief system combinations per meal, per day, per month, per year, per lifetime. Any actions, thoughts, feelings, emotions, smells, location, time, need for approval or love, that occurred during eating created a belief system combination.

If your mother was wearing perfume during the feeding, then, for the rest of your life, the smell of perfume will trigger the belief system to eat even if you just ate.

The belief system combinations condense and multiply and keeps on expanding until every feeling or emotion triggers a eating belief system.

For Instance: food and water

A need for water could trigger a belief system to eat.

Examples

Example A: As a baby, food was a pleasant first experience. Whenever your mother loved or wanted to please you, she gave you food. All celebrations include food. The result is a tremendous combination belief system that says: "When anything anywhere happens that is <u>favorable</u>, eat food."

Example B: When you felt or had a bad experience, your mother gave you food to cheer you up. The belief system formed is, "Whenever anything <u>bad</u> happens anywhere, eat food."

Example C: If you were punished as a child by not being allowed to eat, primitive man will force you to gorge on food whenever you feel you are being punished.

Example D: When you are alone, lonely, depressed, bored, happy, etc., there is that feeling that something is missing. What is it? The belief system answer is food.

Example E: When you are confronted with an unsolvable problem (example, a loved one has an incurable disease), it is too painful to admit and consciously acknowledge that you are helpless, hopeless, and powerless. The bad experience you are having triggers example B and you overeat. This creates action (eating) and gives you the feeling you are doing something about your problems.

In addition, you now feel in control. Whereas you were helpless about the incurable disease, you do not feel hopeless, helpless, and powerless regarding losing weight. After all, you have lost lots of weight in your lifetime.

Furthermore, your overeating is fulfilling another deep belief system, "In order to survive, I must be miserable;" and being overweight is certainly making a big contribution to that. The original eating belief system grows to include incurable diseases.

You eat when you are <u>not</u> hungry because you have belief systems that say the solution to any emotional problem is food. The result is that *any* feeling or combination of feelings can trigger an <u>unconscious</u> craving to eat.

For example:

When I feel deceitful, prim, ugly, nutty, determined, angry, sure, screwed up, exasperated, guilty, obsessed, panicked, confused, vivacious, infatuated, opposed, odd, capable, bold, wicked, vulnerable, concerned, burdened, nice, delighted, eager, good, weepy, rage, fascinated, brave, relaxed, powerless, pitiful, rejected, pressured, mad, reverent, different, discontented, full, frantic, enchanted, depressed, exhausted, horrible, bad, petrified, furious, grief, shocked, glad, settled, evil, charmed, relieved, flustered, greedy, ashamed, worried, silly, great, agonized, I will eat!

Your weight is your report card on your life. The way you present yourself to the world, reflects what you think of yourself. Looking good makes you feel good, attracts the opposite sex and is what a great life is all about. Losing weight is the equivalent of giving yourself a magic wand to create your own happiness. Being overweight is the opposite.

Instant gratification is a one time pleasure that makes you miserable every time you look in the mirror. Normal weight is never ending self-esteem and delight at your appearance. Maintaining <u>overweight</u> requires tremendous energy and constant eating. Little time is leftover to enjoy life. If someone made you do it consciously, you would rebel. What is so powerful that it can force the body against all common sense to stuff itself? Belief systems formed on the level of," near death intensity."

Maintaining normal weight is directly proportional to eliminating belief systems. The more belief systems you lose, the more normal your weight will become.

The ego has millions of belief systems to use against you. When you consider primitive man has been accumulating survival belief systems over thousands of lifetimes, it's hard to imagine the size of the task.

Researchers say that twins raised apart weigh about the same as adults. Why not, they had the same ancestors' belief systems!

If a person weighs 200 lbs., that's 3,200 ounces. If you have a billion belief systems about eating, that equals 312,500 belief systems per ounce!

The Problem

Do you have any memories of observing people eating slow? As children we observed our parents and friends gorging. These belief systems to gorge trigger primitive man'"fear of death" and we go unconscious.

Belief System Concept of Eating is All Wrong

Our belief system concept of eating is all wrong. Do you enjoy reading a good book slow or fast? Are you sorry when it ends? When you encounter beauty in nature, do you take one gulp and turn away or savor the moment for a long time?

Don't Do Anything During Eating You Would Not Do During Sex

With food, we start eating and forget to stop. We swallow our food so fast the taste buds in our mouth never come in contact with the food. How pleasant would intercourse be if the penis never touched the walls of the vagina?

Do you read the paper, listen to the radio, watch television while you are masturbating? Eating involves as much time and attention. Stay conscious when you eat!

The result of eating fast is that the food is not in the mouth long enough for the taste buds to evaluate the food intake and notify the brain to shut down. If you enjoy lobster, eating three pounds in five minutes is not the answer! This behavior can kill. The body becomes overweight, over-stressed, and diseased and you get to be miserable.

The solution is to eat a small amount very slowly and prolong the lobster's contact with the mouth's taste buds as long as possible. Once you swallow, joy ends. To the stomach, all food is work.

The Signal

If a binge of chocolate could end with an orgasm like sex, we would be thin because we would know when it's over. Why do we get a signal in sex but not food?

Our body does give us a signal! Your inner voice talks to you every meal but our belief systems about eating drowns it out. If you stay conscious, it will get louder and louder. You can learn to listen to it.

For instance, you go into a restaurant and order soup and salad. You know soup and salad is good for you. First, you get the soup and, of course, a roll. You meant to eat part of the roll with the soup and the rest with the salad. However, before you know it, the soup is gone and so is the roll.

Now the salad: a little lettuce, some carrots, heart of palm and artichoke, a little turkey, coleslaw, some cucumber slices, a couple pieces of tomatoes, some onions, and a spoonful of dressing to go with it, and another roll. Your plate is overflowing, but, you say, it's all good for you. Right! All three thousand calories!

About one third way through the salad, the voice you say you have never heard says, "enough!" You say, "Are you crazy? I haven't eaten the artichokes and the heart of palm. I paid good money for this. This food is good for me." And you continue to eat.

Twenty minutes later, you're not full, which you would be if you had listened to the voice, but stuffed, uncomfortable, and sleepy. Another belief system is saying, "What the hell, you've gone this far, why not dessert?"

Cause and Effect Cannot Connect

A belief system will not let you visualize the future consequences of a present act. If you could stay conscious, you would say, "If I eat this, I'm going to be miserable!" However, a belief system does not allow consciousness so cause and effect cannot connect.

You will be amazed when you listen to your inner voice how poorly you have been meeting the needs of your body. Stay conscious, you can identify hundreds of interconnected belief system combinations and eliminate them over a few meals.

Your goal is to eliminate enough belief systems to change the balance from slow accumulation to slow return to normal by eating small amounts of food slowly and not letting belief systems make you unconscious. Then you will eat what you want when you want and stop by listening to the signals of the body.

Appetite Mechanism

Food intake continues from the time you put something in your mouth to eat until your appetite mechanism stops sending hunger pains to the brain.

Contained in all processed foods are ingredients to make food taste good. When these nutrients are distilled (sugar cane to sugar), the taste buds in the mouth go crazy and want more of it so it overpowers the stomach's pleas to stop sending food down.

The answer is not sauces, sugar, condiments but chewing the food until the taste reveals itself to the taste buds of the mouth. When you use salt, pepper, sugar, sauces, all the food tastes like the added ingredient.

How does a carrot, pea, bean, potato, celery, apple, taste? Each has a different taste, but you eat so fast and with so many additives you cannot discover this.

How much we eat during this time determines at what weight we will live. You can eat a hell of a lot of food in this interval especially if we go unconscious and primitive man shows up. You overwork the stomach which makes you fat and miserable.

The stomach hunger pains will shut off in 20 minutes even if you only eat one slice of bread.

Craving

When you have a vague craving or desire to eat, a feeling you cannot define, you don't know what the matter is. Exercise doesn't make it go away and you are not hungry. What you are experiencing is a belief system inserted before your memory existed. This belief system is surfacing; but it has no language to communicate to you.

Example: During infancy, you were held while you ate. Therefore, "In order to survive, eat and be held." Your desire to be held is showing up as a desire to eat.

A craving is a clue to an unconscious belief system.   The craving is the result of a triggered belief system. Your body may crave potassium (solution--bananas).   The belief system says, "When I have a craving, eat ice cream." The result is you get ice cream instead of potassium. Furthermore, if we eat a ton of ice cream, the craving for potassium will not go away. The craving for potassium will trigger the belief system and you will eat even more ice cream even though your lips are frozen. All of this goes on unconsciously.

Primitive man controls our eating unless we locate and eliminate the belief systems that trigger him. Throughout history, even now in some places, hunger is a terrible problem. Primitive man has been hungry thousands of times and has died from lack of food.

Talk to primitive man whenever you get the urge to eat; but you are not suffering stomach pain. Ask him why he is upset and afraid he will starve. Tell him about all the food you have in the house and all the money you have to buy more. Make a special visit to the grocery store and show him all the food that is available. Do whatever you feel will calm primitive man down and decrease his fear of starvation. Stay awake during these trips and conversations and your belief systems will surface for you to eliminate.

Chocolate contains Beta-phenylethylamine, a mood lifter. People who are depressed over the break up (rejection) of an intense love relationship frequently gorge themselves on chocolate.

Rejection and the need for chocolate is an excellent opportunity to do a process and not eat the chocolate. Every rejection triggers the original rejection. Go for it! We all have cauliflower hearts because of real or perceived rejection.

Emotional Craving

Emotional cravings sometimes reveal desperate needs for attention, protection, love, approval. Food in the belly can't satisfy the lungs' desire for smoke, loneliness, the feelings that you are unattractive to the opposite sex nor the anxiety and guilt of not being married. In most cases, overeating will increase these problems.

An emotional craving is a belief system that needs a process done on it, not an intake of food. The solution is to remove the belief system. Everybody is attractive without belief systems.

How do you begin?

Commitment

Losing weight takes commitment. If you can't make a commitment, do a process and locate the blocking belief system. Otherwise, you will end up with another failure belief system. Beware of belief systems that say you have no belief system about hunger.

Change your attitude. A day on a diet can be an exciting search for painful, hurtful enemies (belief systems) that once eliminated open the door to a life of joy.

Decide your search for belief systems is more important than anything else; That it's worth all the time even if it involves every minute of every day.

Consciously remember the final result of over eating is being miserable.

What Do You Do Best?

Everyone is talented in some area. Consider for a moment how much knowledge and years of experience you have in your special area. You do it well because you have few if any blocking belief systems. If you knew as little about your special talent as you do about food, what chance of success would you have?

Know as much about food as woman know about cosmetics or men about sports.

Go to the library, read every diet book. Research all information about calories, food, exercise, fats, carbohydrates, sugars, vegetables, chocolate, portions of food. Study labels on cans. Investigate the laws that allow manufacturers to call sugar by different names so you don't realize how much is present.

Correct Eating

PLAN

Correct eating involves consciousness. First, determine it is not an emotional craving.

Define Your Hunger

Consider the following:

1. So hungry you can't move. People have to squeeze liquid food into your body to create life's energy.
2. Same; but you could squeeze the liquid food in yourself.
3. Same; but you want solid food.
4. You could wait another hour to eat if you had to.
5. If you had to stop eating right now, you could but you would miss dessert.
6. You have had dessert. You feel full but your taste

buds want one more dessert.

7.   You're out of control. Your mouth is in charge. You are fully unconscious.

8.   Same; but you're at an "all you can eat restaurant" and it's "you against the house!" You paid $16.50 and you're going to eat $50.00 worth of food even if you have to go home in an ambulance.

9.   Same; but you have left the restaurant and want ice cream. You're so full you feel sick and want to throw up.

10.   Same; but you have eaten a quart of ice cream and either passed out or vomited.

11.   After you vomit, you start eating again and start over at #6.

Before You Eat

You have blocking belief system about starting and staying on the diet. When you get to your normal weight, there will be blocking belief systems about maintaining it.

Every feeling or emotion around the eating process is due to a belief system. They will show up as undefined cravings, not as belief systems.

Ask questions. How much do I want to put on my plate? If I order a full sandwich, can I eat half and doggie bag the rest? What do I want: 1) food--water, 2) sweet--sour, 3) hot--cold, 4) soft--hard, 5) salty, 6) light--heavy, 7) meat--vegetable salad, 8) greasy, 9)crunchy--sticky?

Unlocking Unconscious Belief System Combinations

1.   Why not eat dinner from a saucer? Use a tea table? What are your belief systems about the size of dinner plates, forks, spoons, the table itself?

2.   Do you eat to pass the time? When you have empty time, do you unconsciously look for food? What belief systems do you have about eating and time?

3.   What combines with food and triggers the desire to eat: movies and popcorn, television, a warm fire and hot chocolate, and so on.

4.   Did cleaning your plate in childhood get parental approval and love? Who encouraged you to eat? What belief systems does it trigger? You may eat a huge meal in a restaurant and unconsciously expect the waiter to praise you!

5.   Eat every eight hours. Eat in the dark in the bedroom standing up or outside. Eat one peanut a minute.

6.   Put a sign on the refrigerator ("If I eat this, I'm going to be miserable.") with water inside. Each time you feel a desire to eat but have no hunger pains, mark the paper and drink the water. Do not eat!

Stay conscious and notice what you were feeling or thinking about just before the desire to eat triggered you. Was it boredom, worry, stress, fear, loneliness, sense of loss, overwhelmed, etc.? Write it down. It will become obvious, not only that you do not eat because you are hungry but what belief systems are triggering you.

7.   If you eat alone, eat with someone; if you do not watch TV or listen to the radio do so; if you nibble all day, gorge yourself each time you nibble or, try the reverse.

8.   Write a story about every piece of food you put into your mouth. Why you chose it. Why you ate it, how you ate it, how it tasted. How you felt when you swallowed it. What memories came up? Write the memories down for they are

all belief systems.

9.   Buy two of everything you eat in a week. Examine the amount and analyze why you ate it. What? When? Where? Why?

10.   Imagine a seven-day boating trip. No grocery stores! Plan consciously what you are going to eat each meal. Eat it, brush your teeth, use a mouthwash, go for a walk. Feel how full you are. Notice and acknowledge your feeling and emotions. What past memories come up? Write them down no matter how insignificant.

11.   If you cannot stop eating a certain food (ice cream), change the condition under which you eat it. Change the flavors, buy it at a different store, get a different brand. Refer to your favorite food in an ugly way.

      If you have a craving for a food you feel you cannot control, take the food, sit down, and eat it very slowly with your eyes closed. Bring all your attention to the taste buds in your mouth. What memory comes up? Write it down. It's a clue to the belief system that is creating the craving. Ultimately, you will dissolve it and the vague uncontrollable cravings will disappear.

12.   Don't eat unless you are conscious. Notice if there are hunger pains. Ask your stomach if it wants to digest food now. It will answer, NO! Listen to it. The body hates over-eating. Your ego - brain will justify any food you put into your mouth.

      What is a hunger pain? Can you describe it? Most of us have never gone without food long enough to be hungry. Feelings from the stomach do not mean you are starving. It is not a signal to eat.

      The stomach automatically contracts as the food leaves the

stomach to enter the intestines. Contractions are an opportunity to discover belief systems!

Why can you go to bed hungry and wake up not hungry? Because they were contractions, not hunger pains.

13.   Don't drink a beverage when you eat. It will speed the food into your stomach.

14.   Visit the kitchen, notice your feeling and emotions. What past memories come up? As a child, what belief systems did you form? What were the rules about the kitchen?

15.   All parties' snacks, grocery stores' bars, etc. are belief system booby traps. Unless you stay conscious, you haven't got a chance. A one-year old baby has a better chance walking through a mine field than you have of getting through the day without overeating.

Look for the following belief systems:

- Is food a pastime?
- Is food a hobby?
- If you're fat, you're rich.
- Fat babies are healthy babies.
- Dieting is very hard, boring, painful. If it was easy, everybody would be thin.
- Weight loss is always temporary. I can prove it.
- I will only gain it back anyway. Why suffer? I haven't got the guts.
- My weight problems are inherited--I'm helpless.
- Food will spoil if I don't eat it.
- Thin people are sick people.
- You have to eat everything to get dessert.
- What are your belief systems about portion control?
- Get your money's worth

- It's OK to cheat a little, just this one time.
- Too hard to change the way I think. It's too late.
- I can't stand another failure.
- No more great restaurants, great wine, no head waiters to serve me. It's too hard. I'm giving up the only pleasure I have in life.
- I really don't care how I look.
- Looking good would create a lot of problems for me. New relationship, etc. I would have to get new friends, new subjects to complain about.
- When I lose weight, I attract people of the opposite sex who only desire me for my body, not my true self. It's hard work to sort through the relationships.

Thin People

Never miss an opportunity to observe a thin person eat.

Thin people have <u>strange</u> belief systems:

1. There will always be another meal.
2. Thin people do not eat by the clock. They know they will not starve unless they don't eat for at least a week. They drink water to solve any feelings from their stomach.
3. They do not have to finish what's on their plate.
4. They can eat what they want.
5. Thin people never deprive themselves. They take what they need.
6. They taste every bite of food and <u>never go unconscious.</u>They eat slow and taste everything.
7. Eating is a pleasure of taste and aroma. It is so enjoyable. <u>They stay conscious</u> so as not to miss a bite.
8. They only eat when they are hungry.
9. They only eat until they are not hungry.
10. They eat exactly what they want to eat and no more.

11.   Thin people know immediately when they are full and stop.
12.   Thin people ask themselves if they are hungry after <u>each</u> bite. They stop and get a doggie bag.
13.   If they can't find what they want, they don't eat or wait or find what they do want to eat.
14.   No scarcity of food.
15.   There are no "should", "ought to", etc. in their minds.
16.   They don't care where the food goes that they don't eat.
17.   They have no time limits.
18.   Thin people know very little about diets, calories, fat. They know everything about doggie bags!
19.   They have no explanation or understanding of fat people.
20.   If you offer a thin person food when they are upset, they will give you a puzzled look.
21.   Thin people eat half an ice cream cone.
22.   Thin people do not graze. They don't eat randomly. They know what they want to eat and will not eat a substitute.
23.   They listen to their body and hear it ask for an orange, salad, steak.
24.   Lack of food is not a punishment.
25.   Thin people do not mind eating alone.
26.   They drink water, not soda, etc.
27.   They give themselves permission to eat anything they want.
28.   Their life isn't about weight; they never think about it except if they are hungry. They are involved in new, exciting, and changing things. They are <u>detached</u> from weight.
29.   Thin people would rather be happy than get pity, attention, sympathy, people helping and fussing over them.
30.   Thin people know how to be good to themselves. They buy themselves gifts, massages, flowers. So it's easy to give themselves a thin body. It comes natural.
31.   Thin people have a plan. Thin people think about the next activity, not dessert. They interrupt the plan to eat and return to the plan or project.
32.   Whenever they have a lot to do and need energy, they eat light like fruit or salad, no fats. Being hungry or eating light food creates energy for stressful days. When they are

anxious or upset, they don't eat.
33. Thin people don't even think about food.
34. Thin people do not weigh themselves. If you ask them, they guess what their weight is or tell you about the last visit to the doctor.
35. Thin people are free.
36. Thin people have thin pets.

So, after a few weeks of consciously eliminating belief system, you'll get discouraged because you haven't lost any weight. Frankly, it's not an easy job. You spent your whole life creating these belief systems. It's going to take some time to eliminate them. Stay conscious. It's worth it. Sooner or later, you will eliminate a big one and weight will disappear.

B. SMOKING

It takes about 14 days for your body to give up it's physical need for tobacco. However, many of us have started smoking again after months or years of abstinence. Why?

Even though you have eliminated the physical need for tobacco, you have not eliminated the belief system that causes you to smoke.

Take any time when you felt vulnerable and awkward. This created painful anxiety. At that moment, you had a need to relieve your anxiety and could have done so by saying; "Gee, I feel painfully anxious." You probably would have taken a deep breath and lessened the anxiety.

Unfortunately, few of us were ever taught to handle our emotions that way. Severe anxiety triggered primitive man and a belief system formed that if you want to survive death, smoke a cigarette.

Belief systems are not solutions, but substitutes for the solution.

So what really occurred?

While you were feeling painfully anxious, someone offered you a cigarette. You felt <u>less</u> awkward and vulnerable, because now you were doing something with your hands and your mouth that lessened your anxiety.

Here is where the body creates a belief system that says; Whenever I feel anxious, smoke a cigarette. From that moment on until death, every time you feel anxious, you will smoke. Primitive man feels he will die if he doesn't smoke. Your will power hasn't got a chance under these circumstances.

Furthermore, you were not conscious of when you created the belief system, so you will never know why you smoke. When you feel anxiety coming on, you will avoid it by having a cigarette and the belief system will be buried even more deeply, and until death, you will smoke without knowing why.

Here is a possible example:

A teenager goes to a dance to meet someone. The teenager has a strong desire to be loved and a terrible fear that any request for that love will be rejected. These desires and fears create painful anxiety which the teenager has not been trained to handle.

The correct action is to observe yourself, determine you are anxious, and acknowledge it. Instead, you deny it and continue to feel awkward, vulnerable and anxious. Someone offered you a cigarette and...

Your blood creates smoke cells to dissolve all this smoke. When you give up smoking, it is these smoke cells starving from a lack of smoke that creates the withdrawal pains. It takes about 14 days to starve them and the physical need to smoke to go away.

However, the belief systems regarding anxiety remains. Sooner or later under a condition of extreme and painful anxiety, you will give in and smoke, not because of a physical need, but an emotional one.

Trying not to smoke during a crisis is in effect giving up your defenses against death. Your belief systems are saying you will die if you don't smoke.

When you feel like a smoke, STOP! Do a process on how you feel physically and emotionally. Your belief system regarding smoking will return to consciousness to discover and eliminate.

When smoking belief systems are eliminated, you will not smoke. The body hates smoke.

It is possible by videotaping a meaningful conversion with a smoker to find many clues to his belief systems.

C. ALONE--ALONENESS-LONELINESS

Loneliness

We seek a loving, caring, partner, and fail to find that special one. How can so many people that desire to be together intermingle thousands of times and remain apart? What frustrates this intense need to get together?

We are unaware that we have been accumulating, through unconscious observation, belief systems about every conceivable thing from birth which grow us apart at an increasing rate as we get older: fat--thin, short--tall, rich--poor, young--old, smart--dumb, sensitive--insensitive, wrong race, wrong language, wrong location, wrong religion.

We get together to satisfy our belief systems. Since I don't know yours and you don't know mine, we fail and suffer intense pain.

This intense pain and the need to get together is called loneliness. We must endure this painful situation because we say we have <u>no</u> belief systems. To avoid this pain, we force ourselves to mingle with any available person, seek a mate we don't want and endure horrible marriages and wonder why we feel more empty than full.

People may suggest that you go out and meet other people. Good luck! It doesn't work that way. If you're lonely, the physical world around you doesn't care. It doesn't even know you are lonely. The world is always the way it is. It does not change. Only when you change does it appear to you that the world has changed.

Do processes on loneliness over and over until you eliminate the belief systems that are keeping you lonely! When you do that, the world will not be lonely anymore.

Hot And Cold Relationships

You can usually predict the intensity of the initial relationship by the degree of the preceding loneliness of the people involved. Add to this all the free motherly love we have been doing without since we gave up nursing, and like the song,"It gets too hot not to cool down."

This cool down is miserable to experience and the end result of all belief systems on love. After the bloom is off the rose, all the other belief systems kick in. Each continually finds disappointment in the other. Both are confused and miserable.

Aloneness; Communion with God

Loneliness is aloneness completely covered by belief systems.

Loneliness is a substitute for something else just like a cigarette is a substitute for something else and that something else is communion with God. We try to fill the hole with communion with each other. When we are rejected we experience loneliness and survive thus creating a belief system: "In order to survive, and not experience rejection, be lonely".

The hole inside of us we are trying to fill, is blocked from communion with God by our lifetime accumulation of belief systems

Alone

We all need a moment of solitude to recharge; a time to listen to the silence of our being. When you are conscious, being alone can be a magnificent luxury. A tranquil person will instantly sense the infinite in themselves and in whatever surrounds them.

You are never alone. When you say to yourself that you are alone, to whom are you talking? When you are consciously alone, you are in communion with God. God lives inside us as our self, our essence.

Whenever you acknowledge aloneness, you are experiencing oneness in the present with everything.

Without belief systems, we would realize we are one consciousness. You are I, and I am you. We are everything. What's left is nothing and we can't be lonely for that.

Conscious self-love is the answer to filling the hole created at birth.

D. LOVE

Belief System Love

The love we know is a belief system inserted the same way

as anger, guilt, and grief.

Belief system love is one set of belief systems falling in love with another set of belief systems. One ego loving another ego.

We want our love to conform and confirm our love belief systems (inserted by observation unconsciously). Since a belief system is not real, neither is the love shaped by it.

Belief system love is <u>not</u> a many splendored thing. It is the number one contributor to the Misery Tree. It is part of the trunk and extends to all the branches and leaves.

Falling in belief system love is easy, but doesn't work. Belief system love is for your pets. They can be sent to obedience school. They have no choice but to be dependent, loyal, and never leave us.

The Problem

When you were a baby, everything about you was lovable. When you said the right thing or looked nice, you were loved and you survived. Belief systems formed that say in order to be loved, you have to be lovable, dress well, be attractive. Later you acquired more lovable belief systems about power, sex, or money.

This relentless search for ways to be lovable creates billions of dollars in the selling of dresses and cosmetics. Men work themselves to death acquiring wealth and power. Everyday we stand around like wooden dummies being lovable and bewildered when nothing happens.

Belief systems on love and marriage have a lot to do with society's elders not wanting a bunch of unclaimed children on the streets and is really a trick or form of temporary insanity to trap us into marriage.

"Till death do us part!" What sane person would sign such a contract.

Love people! Be interested in them. Don't make yourself a lovable object. Don't operate out of your childhood belief systems.

Familiarity

The truth is that we marry familiarity.

If a girl and a boy are raised in the same neighborhood, in the same religion and generally exposed to the same environment everyday, mentally and physically, they will possibly have similar, but not identical, belief systems about love. They won't know what they are, or how they got there. If they married and got along well, people would say they are and have been in love.

Where these two people experience different observations, their belief system would differ and conflicts would occur. They will not know any more about what the conflicts are about then why they mostly get along. It's all unconscious.

Belief System Escalation

When the intimacy increases, so does the belief system combinations of the people involved creating confusion and misery. For instance, here is a progressive accumulation.

A boy meets a girl and they become casual friends. Their belief systems combine at a relatively low level. As the relationship becomes more serious, the rate and quantity of belief system combinations intermingling increases.

You have more belief systems about a good friend than a casual friend. A good friend is expected to do more, even if your good friend and you are not conscious of this expectation. If the

Marriage

Hidden Belief Systems

I have the following belief systems
I know nothing about.

1. Man and woman are equal.
2. All decisions should be shared.
3. Large family.
4. Live in city.
5. All religions are the same.
6. Money is not important.

I have the following belief systems
I know nothing about.

1. Man is dominant, woman must adjust.
2. Man makes the decisions.
3. Small family.
4. Live in country.
5. My religion is the only one.
6. Money is important.

Let's get married
I love you
I can't live without you

Good Luck Folks !

The Script

Mother of the Bride

"Your son is so handsome, kind and considerate. I just love him."

Mother of the Groom

"Your daughter is an angel, so sweet and kind. I just love her."

Marriage - **The Clash of**

Sister of the Bride.

I want nothing to do with them.
We have nothing in common.
Ugh, their clothes are horrible.

Brother of the Bride.

I hope he likes baseball
and the Dallas Cowboys.
I'd like to meet his sister.

Father of the Bride.

He's an artist. He can't make a living.
My daughter will starve.
My baby is too young to marry.
Maybe I can bribe them to elope.
I hope he likes the Redskins.
Will they name the first son after me?
Momma Mia, my grandson
will wear a yarmulke!

Grandma

The only way this marriage will work
is if they live in China.
Another damn gift!
What an accent! Are we in Israel?
In two years, He'll be 200 lb slob
full of beer, asleep in front of the T.V.

Cousin Susie

I'm surprised they found each other.
A miracle!
She's very lucky.
The kids will be going to religious
services the whole weekend.

Aunt Mary

It won't last two years.
He's too short for her.
Love is blind.

Mother of the Bride.

My life is the in the toilet
My daughter will go to hell for
marring outside the religion.
He won't be good for her.
What will my friends say?
She'll be a slave.
He'll take advantage of her.
It's a tribe, not a family.
It's best they live near me so
I can take care of them.

Will they help with the
cost of the wedding.

Uncle Joe

Wait until they meet the rest
of the family. They ought to call this
the passport-greencard wedding.
I hope they are not bleeding-heart liberals.
I hope their children do not have his nose. I
wonder if She's pregnant? She did very
well for herself.

The Titans of the Belief System World

Mother of the Groom.

Oy, Vay, why does God hate me?
It will be a cheap wedding.
I will be embarrassed.
All that education wasted.
No class. No taste.
She won't be good to him.
He's so sensitive.
She'll spend his money.
What will my friends say.?
My son is so good looking,
he deserves better.
It's best they live near me
so I can take care of them.

Sister of the Groom

I want nothing to do
with them.They have
no class or taste.
I don't want to be in
this wedding.

Brother of the Groom.

My brother is crazy to get
married.I hope he will be
happy.They deserve
each other.

Father of the Groom

What a mess!
Why couldn't he find an nice girl
that was one of us?
What did I do wrong?
I'll have to pay for half of this
wedding. Will they name the
first son after me.

Grandpa

We'll all be eating spaghetti come
the wedding.
Two can live as cheaply as one, if
one is a horse and the other a bird.
If they're happy, leave it be.
It's a marriage made in heaven.
and that's where they should live!

Uncle Abe

Wait until they meet the rest of the
family. He probably knocked her up.
I hope they are no John Birch people.
What an accent! Are we in Italy?

Aunt Sadie

He did very well for himself.
They deserve each other.
They will have two children.
Love is better than money.
Another damn gift!

couple move up the scale to the dating level, more unconscious belief systems are involved than just good friends. If their belief system do not clash, at this level, intimacy results, with even larger combinations.

Engagement is the major leagues. Belief system integration is immense, involving parents, grand-parents and other relatives, all carrying dissimilar and individual belief systems about love and every conceivable thing that may or may not exist anywhere in the universe.

Then comes the major clash of the titans of the belief system world. The merging of marriage belief systems from all relatives and friends on both sides. (See previous page)

We all have belief systems about how a husband, wife, father and mother-in-law, sisters, brothers, cousins, relatives should behave, all unconsciously inserted by observation, never questioned, or confirmed.

Eye to eye (hand to hand) combat for the egos. For a while, the world seems to go crazy until all the belief systems of all the major players are displayed and considered.

Conscious Love

Conscious eternal love or true love <u>does</u> exist but we are all so covered by belief systems about love that we are kept from ever experiencing it. If we do, we can never realize it because our present belief systems about love will deny it. The real thing doesn't look like, feel like, or act like, what we are all expecting according to our belief systems.

Nothing is as powerful as conscious love. The more conscious knowledge and understanding you accumulate about any activity or person, the more real love you will experience.

When two people work together, to the best of their ability, just for the thrill of it; giving completely, becoming part of the activity, serving others and acquiring additional knowledge to do it better the next time, the degree of their success will be directly proportional to their love for each other. This is true of any unit, whether a family, town, city, or the universe.

When you do this, love and self-love, will coincide.

Conscious Love:

> is a verb.
> *is work!*
> is the glue that holds all the other emotions together.
> is living life at maximum intensity.
> is moment to moment. It exists like a soap bubble. When it breaks, it's gone. When it's over, it's over. By staying conscious, we can create continual bubbles that last forever.
> involves spiritual growth and is as necessary to the soul as food is to the body.
> is being able to listen through your own belief system opinion to what the love object has to say and respond with 100% concentration.
> is taking a risk of offering your love and experiencing the pain of rejection.
> is what's left when you eliminate every belief system. You will feel it. You can't deny it. All is love, oneness, and God.

Belief system love isn't like this. Because of belief system love we suffer other emotions, anger, fear, resentment,etc. People exhaust themselves for, or to get belief system love.

The Father and Mother of all emotions is conscious love. If you exhaust any emotion what's left is conscious love. With conscious love the world would be perfect, and would stay that way.

It is not loss of love that rules you, it's fear of finding out that nowhere-noway does love exist, even eternal love!

Marriage of Commitment

If you want to have children - find a partner you like and feel you can work with over time. Commit to marriage.

Get all the agreements in writing and make sure you understand the responsibility involved in the commitment. This agreement is hard to write and will reveal hidden belief systems on both sides.

Thereafter, their innermost commitment has to be to discover and eliminate what belief systems are creating expectations that are not being met. The elimination of belief systems will create "oneness" and two people who can cooperate with each other in working toward mutually satisfying and agreed upon goals -- like raising children or paying for a house.

Being "in commitment" with each other is better because it provides time to create conscious love and strength to get through the hard times.

Belief system love does not last forever but your commitment can. Most people do not live happily ever after, but can get through the tough times with proper commitment. You can get to love your commitment!

Besides, unless you get rid of your belief systems, you will create the same relationship again. Why waste your time and money separating?

Loving Yourself

The greatest and only love is self-love. If you love you and I am you then you love me. From this you will love everything and everybody.

Start with self-love. Overflow your glass and give the overflow away. Go like hell everyday and love everything and you will experience God because God is love.

Loving yourself should be the easiest thing in the world. Why is self-love tough? Unfortunately our whole lives, we are told to be modest, a team player, not to get a "big head," play it safe, don't brag or stand out, to play down our home runs so to speak. The result of these belief systems is negative self-esteem. It's tough to love yourself under these conditions.

However, you are responsible for your love!

It's hard work to discover and eliminate your belief systems, but the rewards are wonderful. You will learn to love yourself as you become conscious of your own basic uniqueness.

Loving Relationships

Having a loving relationship involves discovering and removing the belief systems preventing two people from merging into oneness.

Try to identify the belief systems you hold regarding relationships:.

> What do you fear about having a mate?
> What parts of a relationship do you reject?
> What are your criticisms of your current relationship?
> What working relationships have you observed lately?
> What previous relationships have you experienced?

What type of relationship would you like to have.
What belief systems are involved in your own
relationships?
What are your fears of rejection?

Love belief systems control every form of relationship we encounter. Story tellers say relationships are like railroad tracks: They stay close forever, but never really touch in a meaningful way. Ever so close and ever so far away. There is no climax, no feeling of completion. The belief system says: "In order to survive, I have to stay close but never touch."

Some relationships are like roads that cross many other roads. The intersections create all the drama, all the meaningful connections, and all the crashes.

Two rivers merge. One is clear, the other muddy. As they merge, you can see from above a clear and a muddy current. The longer they flow together, the more they blend and become one.

Without belief systems there would be one tract, one road and both rivers would be clear before and after merge.

What past relationship did you observe as a child that resembled your current relationship? What belief systems create the drama? The connections? The crashes? Are you still acting it out?

Divorce

Since people play the game of love without any knowledge of the expectations of their respective unconscious belief systems, they are doomed to not have their needs met.

Two people who thought they were as one, discover that they are actually two different structures of belief systems. They will either cling to each other out of fear of the unknown, or separate full of guilt and blame.

The cry of the guilty is, "You don't love me." If you did you would make my belief systems come true even though you have to guess what they are because I don't know anymore than you do. All I know is that I am miserable and it's your fault!

We call this love, even though it is making us miserable.

When belief systems clash and separation seems inevitable, there is no escape except into other belief system soups of misery called alcoholism, resigned desperation, blind acceptance, jealously, lies, deceit, affairs, and guilt.

Trees do not grow in each other's shade. Both people may not be interested in eliminating belief systems. Unequal growth may tend to create problems. Sometimes eliminating a belief system can remove your need for a partner.

If your love is true, you may have to let your love go. True love is like that.

Enjoy your life together; and if or when it's over, do what is right until your commitment is met in full. Thank each other for the good times, learn from it, and go on to what's next for you.

Parents who are divorced still tell their children how to live even though the rules they followed did not work.

E. FREE WILL

Most people hold the opinion that humans possess "free will." We do have the potential. However, most people never use it.

Free will exists in the present. When you operate out of a belief system, a past event is controlling you. Thus there is a automatic response not free will.

You are free when you can observe any event and not trigger an automatic response (belief system). When you observe the world as it is, not as your belief systems make you see it, you will live a life of total insight and love.

F. DEATH

Everybody wants to go to heaven, but nobody wants to die. Two opposing belief systems that exist in almost all human beings.

No one knows, but we have belief systems inserted inside us that tells us what death is. We cannot consciously fear death because no one has ever experienced it and "lived to talk about it!" What we fear is our belief systems about death.

Near Death Experience

The closest anyone comes on this earth to knowledge about death is a "near death" experience. This is an experience where a person dies (clinically dead) but somehow returns to life. We call it a "near death" experience if we don't die but live on to tell others about it.

In a "near death" experience, people leave their bodies and observe themselves in the death scene from above. They do not feel the pain of the event that created the "near death" experience, yet they see and hear what is happening. Simultaneously, they observe a friendly, fond, welcoming light and are drawn to the warmth of it. They are given the choice to follow the light (death) or return to life. People who return never fear death again. They become spiritual but not religious.

What we do know from people who have had "near death" experiences is that it is very pleasant and certainly nothing to fear. In thousands of reported cases, there has never been a mention of hell.

We could review our total past life if we could trick the body into believing it was dying similar to the conditions existing during "near death" experiences. However, no one has been able to simulate this experience without real danger of death.

Eternal Consciousness

People who believe in eternal consciousness explain and describe death in many ways.

Here are a few:

Does the caterpillar die when the butterfly is born or is he alive in the butterfly?

Or perhaps we are all leaves on a "conscious tree." In the fall, just before the leaves fall to earth, the leaves' consciousness (sap) returns to the tree until spring when it enters a new leaf.

At different times, all of us were an infant, a child, a teenager. Are they now part of your adult life or are they dead?

Millions of cells in our body die and are replaced each day. Ultimately, none of the cells we were born with exist; but we do. What is it that still exists?

The human race exists but no one that composed the human race 200 years ago does or are they conscious inside us and we haven't discovered a way to communicate with them yet?

You and I have already experienced death, the death of the fetus. If you were the fetus and you are dead, how can you be alive right now? Are we dead right now and think we are alive?

If being conscious is being alive, then being unconscious is not being alive. Is a boxer knocked unconscious alive or dead?

If a person is unconscious because of belief systems, who is more alive? A dead person free of belief systems or a live person full of belief systems?

Perhaps the consciousness in our bodies is similar to our behavior towards cars. We exchange our car every few years to something better and more suitable.   A car will last forever, and if it did, we would all be driving slow moving Model T's, without air conditioning, or AM/FM radios. Perhaps our consciousness changes bodies the way we change cars.

Belief systems cause stress which causes parts of the body to self-destruct. When enough parts fail, your consciousness is forced to get a new body. Would you care to be walking around in the body of a prehistoric man or woman right now?

If we are truly one consciousness, past, present, and future, then death is merely a change of state from ice to water to steam.

Why not believe that death is a transition back to eternal consciousness?

Since we don't know, why suffer any anxiety about it? We do not have any past memory of what it was like before we became a human being, so why should we fear going back there? Maybe it's a great place.

Forget about death, it just makes you miserable.

Personally, I intend to enjoy my death. I feel death is an invitation to a great reunion party where all my cosmic friends are waiting to see me. I love parties and I'm curious what other senses there might be.

It is my intention to remain as conscious as I can when I die. I want to see the Buddha or the Lighted Christ and meet my Guides. If not, what have I lost?

Think about all your experiences regarding death. Pick the worst or most traumatic memory about death and do a process on it. If an earlier memory comes up, reexperience that one. Sooner than you think, the negative energy on death will go away.

Gene System

Our gene system is a survival system. Belief systems are the minor leagues for genes. Deeply entrenched belief systems, created at the level of survival, passed on over thousands of years, good or bad, will be assumed to be necessary and will be programmed into the gene pool.

If belief systems are a form of temporary genes being auditioned for long term survival by the gene pool, let us make sure worry, war, hate, guilt, anxiety, murder, and slavery do not make it.

By finding belief systems in your own life and realizing that you are triggering new ones everyday, you set up opportunities to neutralize specific belief systems that totally dictate your behavior.

Is Sleep a Belief System?

The "sleep" gene may be a partial death. At present, except for a "near death" experience, death is the only way for consciousness to escape from belief systems. Sleep may be an instrument to disengage your belief systems so your consciousness can temporarily communicate with the collective conscious universe.

Is sleep a belief system to relieve boredom? Perhaps we were never meant to sleep or die. Fear of the dark forced primitive man into caves until dawn. They were bored and hypnotized themselves into a comatose state to help the time pass. Over eons of time, sleep entered into our genes.

Depressed people are loaded with belief systems and sleep a lot. Alcoholics may pass out for the same reason allowing consciousness to penetrate the heavy belief system cover.

Consciousness may endure death, sleep, drugs or alcohol to escape belief systems and physical bondage so it can communicate with the cosmos.

Death: A Cosmic Pause

Perhaps the death process is a cosmic belief system exam, purification and evaluation center, where each consciousness's acquired belief systems are condensed and processed.

This center could also evaluate the frequency of certain belief systems, whether it helps, and so on. The big repeaters become part of the collective genetic code.

Perhaps this center is necessary because some belief systems are so compacted that it is necessary to convince the individual consciousness that it has survived while the body has not before another life journey can begin.

Live fish in <u>dark</u> underground caves grow membranes over their eyes. Since they don't use their eyes, they lose their eyes. We still have consciousness and the ability to eliminate belief systems. However, belief systems are what we use most of the time and not consciousness. Will membranes grow over our consciousness?

History will depend on whether the human race creates a collective belief system that says, "In order to survive, we must have belief systems" and if so, we will be doomed.

G. HUMOR

Humor is a belief system. The degree of laughter tells you the depth and intensity of the belief systems. Tell me what a person laughs at and I will tell you the areas of their anxieties.

Laughter feels so good because it temporarily relieves anxiety from unconscious accumulated belief systems.

Let's take sexual anxiety. Its big area for laughter and tension release. Comedians love it for that reason.

The comedian relates a story which triggers belief systems and creates tremendous anxiety in the listener. Then the comedian releases the anxiety with a punch line and everybody laughs with relief. A good time for all.

Here is a sexual tension joke:

Judge to Defendant: "You are accused of making love to a dead woman!"

Defendant: "How was I suppose to know, your honor? She was my wife!"

Explanation:

Married couples over time, if unable to communicate their sexual needs, develop guilt belief system about who's fault it is. The tension that the fault might be theirs accumulates over time. The men in the audience laugh because this confirms in their mind that their wives are at fault. Their laughter is conscious but the reason it's so funny to them is unconscious. They feel vindicated and relieved. The women in the audience are so glad that it is not they that are being discussed, that they too laugh in relief. Others will laugh to hide the fact they don't know what is funny about such a sad state of affairs.

Joke:

Joke Teller: (male) "Why did God invent woman?

Answer: Because sheep can't cook!

Joke:

Joke Teller: (male)   "Why do women have more trouble having orgasms than men?"

Answer: Who cares?

Explanation:

A male child is born of and raised by a woman. Woman rule, love, and serve the male child years before memory. Warm, loving, dependent belief systems are created.

Later, a male child observes "macho man" and belief systems about dominance are created.

The result is constant conflicting unrelieved tension.

Joke:

Comedian: Are there any Polish (Italian, etc.) people in the audience?

Answer: Yes? OK, I'll speak slower.

Joke Teller: What do you say to a Spic (Chink, Wop, Pole, Hebe, Black, etc.) in a three piece suit?

Answer: Will the defendant please rise.

Explanation:

Both jokes deal with belief system about inferiority. Many people secretly feel they do meaningless, repetitive jobs that almost anyone, given the opportunity, could also do. People search for reasons why they really make a difference in their world and seldom find comfortable answers. This creates tension.

It would take a separate book to analyze all the variations of belief systems involved in jokes. I'll let you experiment with the idea.

Self-analyze what belief systems was behind the last three jokes that made you laugh.

Belief Systems and Humor

Most people find humor delightful; but be aware, it can be used as a weapon for or against you. If you have ever been the butt of a joke, you will know what I mean. (Being upset because you are the butt of a joke is a belief system.)

A belief system that people laugh at has no power. Status quo power has no need for laughter because laughter dissolves fear belief systems; and without fear, blind obedience is impossible.

Suggestions

Notice what you laugh at (connect it to a memory.)
Notice what your friends laugh at.
Are you a joke teller? Why?
What jokes offend you? Why?
What kind of jokes do you like? Why?

As a child, I discovered that whenever I amused people by making them laugh, I felt love and approval. Any child will gravitate to these positive feelings, unless a belief system blocks it. As a result, I developed a belief system that says; "If you want to feel love and approval from others, make them laugh."

Unconsciously, I accumulated a vast reservoir of material as well as a talent for relating it. Eventually, it became a belief system completely out of control. I told jokes whenever I needed love and approval, not only when it was appropriate. When I became conscious of this belief system, I made some minor changes. Now, I'm <u>conscious</u> of my ability to tell jokes, choose appropriate times, and still receive love and approval.

I observed when I needed love and approval and looked for the belief system involved. By doing this "process," I am able to consciously identify my belief systems regarding jokes and increase my consciousness in this area.

Laughing at a joke is an act of consciousness. You cannot be partially somewhere else.

H. FEAR

Why does fear of the unknown frighten us? As a child, if we were frightened and it ended happily, we did not form a belief system. However, if something harmful happened, and we survived, we created a belief system about fear and survival.

Fear of not being loved, getting angry or being stupid are belief systems. You were not born with these fears.

Suppose you fear that you are unlovable. To be unlovable is very painful. To replace your fear of not being lovable, you create a belief system. The belief system replaces and avoids the pain of feeling not lovable. However, the belief systems will make you miserable.

Consider for example:

A mother constantly criticizes and denies love to a child. The child cannot understand or bear the pain of this unlovable abuse without cause and creates a belief system to avoid it. Her fear of not being loved is replaced by a belief system that says, "I am not loved because I'm a hellion!"

Now when she is abused and denied love, she can say it's because she is a hellion, not because she in unlovable. Whenever this person feels unloved in the future, all hell will break loose.

A fear belief system will replace a denied longing for love. An anger belief system will mask that fear. He will get angry rather than discuss his need for love. He will survive without love and create a belief system, "In order to survive, I must do without love." Belief systems never end. You were not born with these fears.

If you fear something, stay conscious! Many fears can be quickly eliminated by conscious action. If you fear your neighbors, meet them. Bring them cookies. If you are afraid of someone, tell them.

Books tell us that love is an absence of fear; you can conquer fear by praying, meditating, logic, etc. But, you first have to locate why or what makes you afraid.

There is conscious and unconscious fear. Conscious fear, you can work on. Unconscious fear makes you be afraid and you don't know why.

If you were robbed and raped and fear it happening again, that is a conscious fear. If you are afraid of darkness and don't know why, then you are being controlled by an unknown force (belief system).

Here are some fears.

Fear of	Conscious	Unconscious
Motion	Yes	
Future	No	X
Loss of Control	No	X
Physical Relations	No	X
Sex	No	X
Choice	No	X
Death	No	X
Decision	Yes	
People	No	X
Alone	Yes	
Burdened	Yes	
Love	Yes	
Helpless	No	X
Hopeless	No	X
Powerless	No	X
Unworthy	No	X
Victimized	Yes	
Unknown	No	X
Wrong	No	X
Humiliation	No	X
Do Processes	No	X

I. HATE, RESENTMENT, FORGIVENESS

Hate

You hate what you fear.

Common friends as well as common enemies can share hatred. Hatred brings all kinds of people together by smothering dividing emotions.

Feeling of self-contempt, inadequacy, cowardice, worthlessness, guilt, all shortcomings, can vanish and reappear in one big hate for an external object or foe. People seeking to escape from themselves join together and reinforce each other. The self-hate is redirected outward. They join "us against the world" movements. (See Chapter 11: Surrendering to an ISM, Page 107)

This hate belief system appears <u>not</u> only to eliminate self-hate, but self itself. But, the hate remains inside you. You cannot hate without carrying hate inside you.

Suggestion:

If you hate, do processes on self-contempt. When did you hate yourself the most?

Resentment

A resentment upset in most cases, is very easy to find. Most people know what and who they resent, but will not forgive even though its killing them. They have basic belief systems that say it cannot be forgiven and still live a valid life. It means accepting everything they have been against their whole life.

Long term resentment can cause cancer and other illness by creating constant stress. The body cannot fight stress and protect against disease at the same time.

Resentment is where you punish yourself for crimes committed against you! You assume the punishment of the person that made you the victim. You carry the smoldering ill will for the other person inside you. **While you are letting the resentment kill you, the other person is out dancing.**

While you are resenting good things happening to another, you have no time to create good things for yourself.

In the final analysis , we are all victims. Holding a grudge hurts you, not the bad guy.

Resentment comes from a violation of an early and deeply held belief system.

Examples:

> All parents should be, perfect, kind, considerate, love and
>   cherish their children
> Children should take care of their parents.
> People should not be insulted, snubbed or ignored.
> Husbands and wives should not cheat on each other.
> Marriage is forever!

Forgiveness

Forgiveness is the solution to hate and resentment.

In general, we have no idea how to forgive. Our culture has many examples of getting even and holding grudges for centuries. As children, do we ever observe our parent or other adults resolving resentment? Credit and recognition is given to those who get even. Look at the behavior of our leaders. They reflect us.

By discovering the event(memory) that caused the belief system formation, you can consciously investigate and understand the difference between the true event and the way you interpreted the event.

Understanding the total event from all sides including the belief systems of the people involved is the path to resolvement.

Example

Your parents were wrong for the way they raised you, and they have to admit it before you can go on with your life.

You are absolutely right;   They did raise you wrong!

However, did you ever consider what kind of parents they had? Based on their belief systems they are not wrong and if you had their belief systems you would have done it the same way.

Carrying resentment and waiting for them to admit they were wrong will ruin you life. Furthermore, the more you resist, the more the resentment will grow inside you.

When you understand the belief systems of the people involved, tolerance and forgiveness is immediate.

Suggestions

Look for upset regarding betrayal where people you trusted let you down. Where do you seek revenge?

J. GUILT

Imagine the change in the world if you could eliminate guilt in every person's life.

Even if you lead a blameless life, you cannot avoid the collective guilt for living in a society free of poverty, brutality, starvation, and for being better off than other people. We are all caught in the web of guilt. For some people, to be alive is to feel guilty.

Unconscious Guilt

How do you control a person who is happy and at peace with himself? How do you motivate him to do what you want him to do instead of what he wants to do? How do you turn him away from the joys of life, the water, grass, animals, enjoying the breeze, seeing the stars, and all that is available by being consciously aware? The answer is unconscious guilt.

Unconscious guilt is inserted deep and early by people who

wish to control. Their belief systems, decide we are imperfect and should feel guilty. We are too young to object to this insertion.

Another inserted belief system says, if you are guilty, you should be punished. Unconscious guilt seeks physical and emotional pain according to the inserted belief system. One creates stress which causes cancer. Another causes heart trouble. Some just create a car accident. So, you punish yourself by being miserable all the time.

Unconscious guilt brings vitality to a halt, drives people to perform without asking why and makes the world work for the powers that be. It creates sin and punishment. Your guilty conscience comes from this area.

A guilt belief system gives you the feeling you are being isolated, browbeaten, and suffocated, without help and no escape.

If you avoid punishment by doing what authority wants, you feel unfulfilled and lack vitality. Guilt without relief causes intense emotional stress.

God's Way

Nature's way is God's way. We are animals and a rule to follow in this regard is, "If you see an animal doing something that would make you feel guilty if you did it, it's man made!" It's an unconscious guilt belief system." Eliminate it and a life of natural vitality will reveal itself to you.

Conscious Guilt and Free Will

Animals do not have conscious free will but they do have an understanding with nature. Animals possess an innate restriction against excesses such as killing more than they need or eating too much. When an animal experiences pain, the animal heeds the warning and stops whatever it is doing. Originally, this was nature's way of protecting all living beings from one generation to the next.

With free will, the innate restriction against excesses is replaced by a conscience. A conscience's function is to monitor and control "free will" using conscious guilt.

Conscious guilt has nothing to do with sin, sex, or adultery.

Conscious guilt is the wisdom of the ages. It tell us how to coincide with the justice and integrity of the universe. It gives us an opportunity to reflect, just before an action, the future consequence of that action by remembering the consequences of similar past action.

Unconscious guilt prevents this reflection. Conscious guilt is to your conscience what pain is to your body. It is a warning signal that what you are doing is violating nature's laws.

Conscious guilt measures the human suffering taking place. Therefore, a human being using conscious guilt as a measuring guide would understand that his actions have an effect on every thing. His responsibility to himself would be to protect the whole of humanity. When he steals or kills, he steals and kills from himself. We are all one consciousness and hurt ourselves when we hurt anyone else.

Man's conscience was set against itself. Nature did not intend you to be punished because of guilt. Its function was to measure responsibility for our actions which are automatic in animals.

This conscious tool nature gave us can be regained by eliminating your unconscious guilt belief systems.

Core Guilt

If you are guilty about anything, then "anything" isn't the problem. The core belief system is "you believe you should be guilty." All the "anythings" cling to the core guilt belief system. Rid yourself of the core guilt belief system and all the anythings you are guilty about will disappear.

Identify all the times you feel guilty and why. Do processes with other people who feel guilty. When you're doing a process, a deep breath is your clue that you are making progress.

Furthermore, you don't have to understand it. Just identify your guilt as accurately as possible and do a process. You will not understand why the guilt has left you, but who cares as long as it is gone.

We have lost the natural protection instinct gave us. We have covered, its replacement, conscious guilt, with belief system guilt. Belief system guilt has replaced free will.

Guilt-Born Again

True confession is an act of consciousness at the moment of confession. If you were a computer, the _real_ you would be on the screen ready for instructions and corrections.

A "Born Again" meeting says that if you confess, you will not be punished. You feel wonderful because by bringing your guilt into consciousness, you relive it and it disappears.

People who have had a "BORN AGAIN" experience state that at the moment of confession,----"God entered my body and I felt wonderful."

I don't know what entered their body, but I know a guilt belief system left their body allowing more consciousness to be present. If consciousness is everywhere and in everything, perhaps God did not enter but was always inside covered by a guilt belief system.

Consciously confessing the original guilt recreates the experience when the first guilt belief system was inserted and simultaneously allows you to reexperience and eliminate what created the belief system. As mentioned, reliving the event can cause the guilt to disappear. The confessor feels great.

K. PRIDE

Somewhere in your past, a belief system was inserted that said certain acts of behavior were disgraceful and people who do these things are bad. As a result, you fell out of love with yourself, which was painful. To avoid the pain, you inserted a belief system called pride. Pride is a belief system that masks the pain of humiliation. It slips in the same way the person started to smoke.

Look for humiliation in your early life. Search your memory for events that caused you tremendous humiliation and do processes.

L. WORRY

Worry is a first class ticket to the misery tree. It's like taking an extra suitcase filled with lead on a trip. It's of no value and a terrible burden to carry.

Worry in itself is so powerful it can keep you unconscious and miserable without the help of any other belief systems. If it was money, we would be billionaires. It breeds on itself.

You can worry about anything, even about having nothing to worry about. You can worry for a solid year and not change anything. No one can be secure enough not to worry, so it's possible to worry endlessly. It can be a way of knowing you exist. You worry and survive. Therefore, to survive, I have to worry.

Worry Tree

Worry about cancer.   Worry about hot water.
Worry about food spoiling.   Worry about bus being late.
Worry about relationships.   Worry about things being too good.
Worry about clean socks.   Worry about future. or past.
Worry about loss of job.   Worry about Parents.
Worry about getting old.   Worry about death.
Worry about children.   Worry about going bald.
Worry about not being pretty.   Worry about being overweight.
Worry about sanity.   Worry about what they may think.
Worry about good becoming bad.   Worry about getting fat.   Worry about God.
Worry about husband leaving.   Worry about what suit to wear.
Worry about heaven. hell. sin.   Worry about bathroom not working.
Worry about loss of status.   Worry about not doing enough with life.
Worry about refridgerater breaking.   Worry about heart attack. or stroke.
Worry about worrying.

**Basic problem is that you have
a major belief system that says,
"You can not survive without worrying".**

Worry is a normal concern out of control.

It comes from the belief system that you are powerless.

Here are some suggestions:

> Connect every worry to a memory.
> Create a file and as a worry comes up, write it down and file it.
> Choose an hour each day to visit the file and worry intensely.
> Don't worry any other time.
> Notice how little of what you worry about ever happens.

Ask yourself, "If I was going to die in one week, would I worry about that?" This question will allow you to gain some perspective over what you worry about. Certainly, worrying about whether the bus is going to be late is not very important in relation to your death.

When you feel a worry coming on, search for a memory when you were powerless.

You are traveling from birth to death. You will arrive whether you worry or not.

M. SUCCESS

What is success?

We have personal belief systems that tell us what success is. Write down your definition of success. Does it include great wealth, power, position, intellect, beauty? At what price?

Success is looking in the mirror each morning and consciously knowing you have *inner integrity* regardless.

Inner integrity will not make you miserable.

N. RISK

During a seminar, the leader told a story of a child who received constant love and approval for his drawings. The more the child drew, the more praise he/she received. The child liked the approval, love, and praise and decided to get a lot more of it by drawing on the living room wallpaper rather than small pieces of paper.

In the child's mind, the end result was worth the risk. Unfortunately, his parents did not see the drawing but the expense of the ruined wallpaper. The child was severely punished and formed a belief system, "Whenever I take risk, I get severely punished."

My mind flashed a forgotten childhood memory. When I was approximately four years old, my parents spent whatever savings they had accumulated on a porch. During the course of this event, I learned to use a hammer and nail and delighted my parents by hitting nails into pieces of scrap wood. I was intoxicated with their rare approval and love.

I decided to drive nails into the porch. Since I wasn't very good at driving nails, I missed a lot and really banged up the new porch. However, I couldn't wait to show my parents and tingled inside anticipating their delight, love, and approval.

I was brutally punished!

My whole life was filled with fear at the slightest risk. I would sweat, be anxious, and upset and avoided risk whenever possible. All of which became clear to me in that instant!

A risk is a commitment. It creates vulnerability and ridicule if failure results. Taking a risk means jumping into the unknown.

However, take a look at your belief systems regarding risk for they are probably blinding you to paths that have little risk at all and would be beneficial to you.

Risk Taking Logic

BY THE LAW OF NUMBERS EACH RISK HAS A 50% CHANCE OR SUCCESS. BY CONSCIOUS ANALYSIS YOU CAN INCREASE YOUR CHANCE OF SUCCESS AT LEAST ANOTHER 25%. THEREFORE YOU SHOULD BE FAVORABLY INCLINED TO RISK.

O. SACRIFICE

Sacrifice is painful giving from scarcity. People that sacrifice have a belief system that they have to give whether they want to or not. This makes them miserable. You cannot give from an empty cup.

Examples:

Mother to child   I sacrificed for you. I suffered the pain of child birth; I gave up my life, nice clothes, and pleasure so you could have life. The child is helpless - it didn't ask to be born, it can only endure the torture.

Husband to wife   I sacrificed everything for you. What is the wife to do? She wanted to get married and have a family. She never asked anyone to sacrifice.

                             Conversely, a wife that tolerated this torture has a belief system that says, "In order to survive I have to suffer torture."

                             How many couples do we all know where one person is obviously sick and the other tolerates the behavior?

In the first example, the child is helpless and tortured and creates a belief system that says, "In order to survive, I must endure being helpless and tortured." This child grows up to be the wife in example #2 because that life is familiar.

Beware of people who sacrifice. Their unconscious belief system says that in order to survive they must torture people. The sacrifice is the mask to conceal the torture. This belief system creates a sadist. What is familiar for them is to torture people.

Look out for words like service, favor, duty. Behind those words, there is a sacrificer looking to torture you emotionally and physically.

Without belief systems, a mother with a new born baby gives her whole life willingly to the child. The mother would laugh at the notion that she was making a sacrifice. It's giving from abundance. Fill your cup; what overflows, give to others.

List the greatest sacrifices you have made. Do processes.

P. ILLNESS

Illness is a warning that you are destructing your body. Hear it sooner rather than later. Cancer and heart attacks are terminal warnings. A nervous breakdown, headaches, pain in chest, and hemorrhoids, are early warnings that something is wrong.

The natural state of the body is wellness. Illness is a departure from being well. If you have become ill, it is a giant clue that your belief systems have achieved a dangerous and lethal control over you. Your illness is reflecting your inner turmoil created by inserted belief systems.

Be your illness. Notice the location. Go to that part of your body and ask it to tell you about the belief system out of which it is operating.

Is it near your sexual organ? What belief system do you have about sex? Have you been divorced? Do you feel guilty? Do you feel you should be punished? Is the illness your way of punishing yourself? How were you punished as a child?

Watch out for combinations:

"I'm ill and feel bad, therefore I am bad and should be punished by getting more ill."

Q. LAZINESS

Nobody is lazy. We appear lazy because we have belief systems telling us to be. It is a belief system that has to be eliminated.

A disadvantaged, unsuccessful, out of work minority person is not lazy. He has been covered with belief systems his whole life that tell him he cannot be a success; so he, therefore, cannot be successful unless the belief systems are eliminated.

Many people appear lazy after becoming moderately successful. An example is a person more successful than his father. After getting two levels above his father, his incentive evaporates. He doesn't get lazy, he just does not have belief systems to handle more growth.

His belief systems say to be successful, you rise two levels above your father. Another belief system says when you are successful, you take it easy.

Belief systems rob people of vitality and creativity.

Another view is from the difficulty people have who become

rich through series of unexpected events. These people were raised by poor parents and belief systems about being rich were not inserted.

Furthermore, they might have belief systems that rich people are dishonest, untrustworthy, or lacking in integrity. Their belief systems about politics may be aligned with poor people. They may have complained a great deal about the rich uncaring people in charge; and now, they are the rich uncaring people. There is no familiarity with this class of people.

Without belief systems to handle all this, tremendous, painful laziness (lack of action) and anxiety will result. Alcohol, drugs, and deliberate loss of wealth can be the aftermath.

R. WAR AND SLAVERY

There are no warlike people, just warlike belief systems.

Millions of people have been murdered during wars because they held different belief systems. Yet, most societies justify war.

War and slavery belief systems are as old as mankind and initially were very useful in the survival and the welfare of the winners. They have now become a threat to the species. Nuclear war does not benefit the winner, but we are still operating out of a belief that says it will.

When any belief system states that one thing is more important than another, war, slavery and killing is inevitable. Hate, envy, pride, fear, lies, terror, greed, power, and hunger cause wars among people, families, and nations.

We inherit belief systems passed down over many lifetimes that say the survival solution to these problems is war and slavery. The modern day person inside us shouts for peace but our prehistoric belief systems tell us the answer is war and slavery.

Prehistoric belief systems about war and slavery survival, if not eliminated, will create our destruction.

Many of our belief systems come from man observing the animals. If animals killed each other with impunity, why not do it too? When man fought an animal or another man, and survived, a belief system was formed: "In order to survive, I have to kill."

How did we end up with belief systems that it's OK to kill animals for meat, but not each other? When in time did we make the distinction?

When was the slaughter house invented? Did one tribe capture another for food? Were they put in cages and fed until needed? Have we stopped killing each other or just stopped eating each other?

Consider the similarities in belief systems about war, slavery, dog and cock fighting, burning witches, and molesting children?

The War and Slavery areas are great sources of hopeless, helpless, and powerless belief systems. The magnificent truth is that we are not hopeless, helpless, and powerless. Every time we eliminate a personal belief system, we also decrease the unconscious collective belief system area in all areas including war and slavery.

Chapter 16

GLOBAL HUNGER

Global hunger, a major cause of war, would lessen if we had different belief systems about meat. For example, here are four belief systems that contribute to world hunger that should be examined:

Rich people eat more meat than poor people.
Eating meat three times a day means you are rich.
Vegetarians are weird people.
Killing animals for food is a good and practical solution.

About 50% of the world's grain is used to fatten animals. The same land used to grow soya products would yield 20 times more usable protein. South America is presently converting its rain forest to grazing land. About 40% of the world's oxygen comes from rain forests. If we ate less red meat, it would help a lot.

Conference To Decide The Issue Of Abortion.

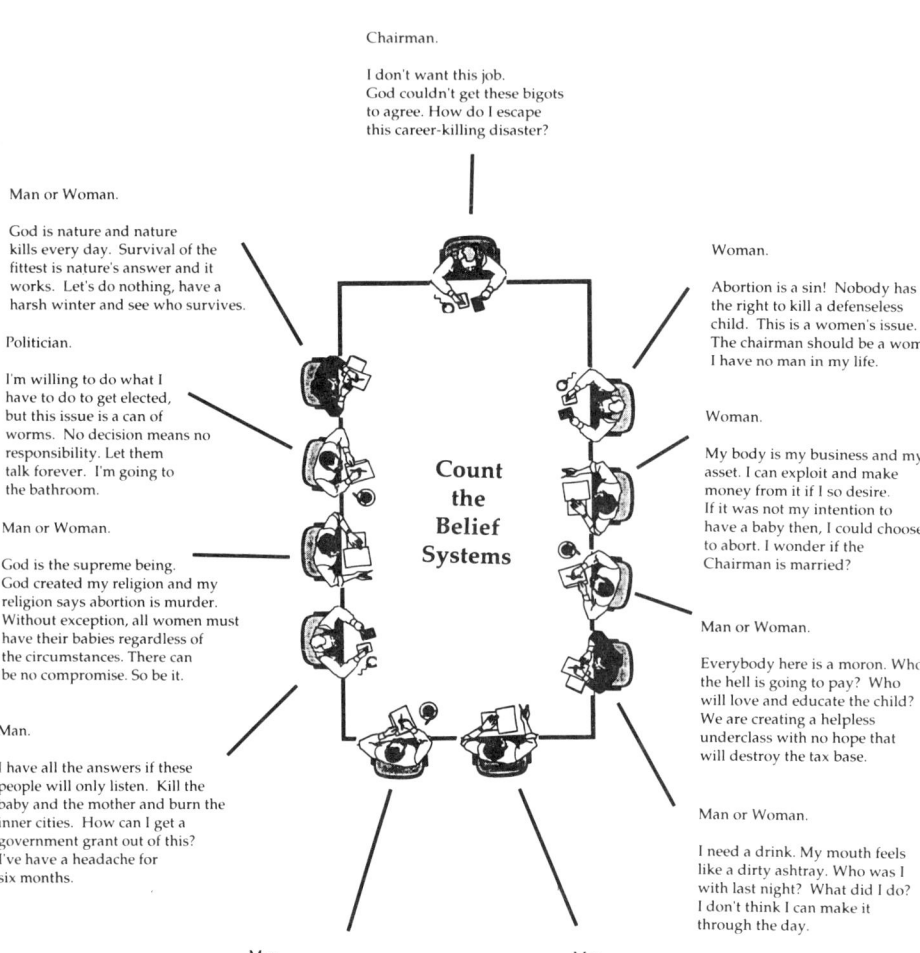

Chairman.

I don't want this job.
God couldn't get these bigots
to agree. How do I escape
this career-killing disaster?

Man or Woman.

God is nature and nature
kills every day. Survival of the
fittest is nature's answer and it
works. Let's do nothing, have a
harsh winter and see who survives.

Politician.

I'm willing to do what I
have to do to get elected,
but this issue is a can of
worms. No decision means no
responsibility. Let them
talk forever. I'm going to
the bathroom.

Man or Woman.

God is the supreme being.
God created my religion and my
religion says abortion is murder.
Without exception, all women must
have their babies regardless of
the circumstances. There can
be no compromise. So be it.

Man.

I have all the answers if these
people will only listen. Kill the
baby and the mother and burn the
inner cities. How can I get a
government grant out of this?
I've have a headache for
six months.

Woman.

Abortion is a sin! Nobody has
the right to kill a defenseless
child. This is a women's issue.
The chairman should be a woman.
I have no man in my life.

Woman.

My body is my business and my
asset. I can exploit and make
money from it if I so desire.
If it was not my intention to
have a baby then, I could choose
to abort. I wonder if the
Chairman is married?

Man or Woman.

Everybody here is a moron. Who
the hell is going to pay? Who
will love and educate the child?
We are creating a helpless
underclass with no hope that
will destroy the tax base.

Man or Woman.

I need a drink. My mouth feels
like a dirty ashtray. Who was I
with last night? What did I do?
I don't think I can make it
through the day.

Count
the
Belief
Systems

Man.

When is the lunch break?
I've got a date with a knockout!
I wonder if I can get her in the
sack tonight? What are these
people talking about anyway?

Man.

My kids won't talk to me and my
wife won't shut up. I'm in
love with another woman. My
margin account is $10,000.00 short
and I haven't got it. I can't pay
my bills and the bank is going
to repossess my house.

Chapter 17

DECISION MAKING

Why does a crisis have to happen before anything gets done?

If you are convinced that we all have belief systems, then you can begin to understand why decisions among people, religions, politicians, and governments are so difficult.

All groups trying to make a decision are operating out of their personal belief systems. Until we can discover and eliminate belief systems from each person regarding the topic under discussion, no agreement is possible, and we will suffer terrible pain.

A politician will do what will get him re-elected. What that is, more often than not, is a mystery to him. How can anybody know what people full of belief systems wants?

The politician needs group agreement or a "oneness". A "oneness" can only exist without belief systems. A crisis creates a "oneness."

A gasoline crisis creates a oneness about doing whatever has to be done to make gas more available. Thus, the politician has group agreement to make gasoline available at any price at no risk to his political future.

In America, when we have a new idea, because of belief systems, we cannot decide consciously, so we vote on it. The politicians do not count our votes but our belief systems, because we automatically and unconsciously vote our belief systems.

If you study the abortion issue, you will soon discover everyone is operating out of belief systems. The abortion issue will be decided politically, not ethically.

It will take 100 years to settle it ethically when the deeply inserted belief systems of this era are eroded away similar to ideas like "the world is flat," "there cannot be objects in the sky," and "the earth is the center of the universe."

Conflicts can be resolved by eliminating belief systems, not winning. Mikhail Gorbachev eliminated his belief system about communism and the Berlin Wall came down!

We are polluting the air and creating less of it. There was more of it in ancient times. Brains function better with proper amounts of 02. Pollution is destroying our awareness.

When earth people begin to choke, a oneness about eliminating pollution will occur.

PROCESS

RETURN PATH TO ORIGINAL UPSET:

←

**EXPERIENCE PRESENT UPSET TO
DISCOVER EARLIER UPSET AND/OR
ORIGINAL UPSET**

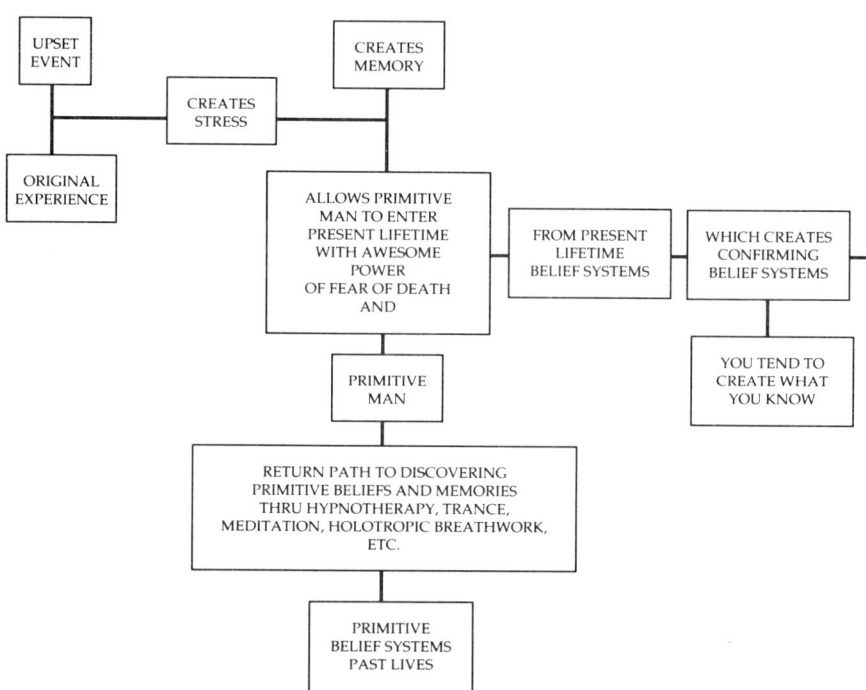

UPSET
EVENT

CREATES
MEMORY

CREATES
STRESS

ORIGINAL
EXPERIENCE

ALLOWS PRIMITIVE
MAN TO ENTER
PRESENT LIFETIME
WITH AWESOME
POWER
OF FEAR OF DEATH
AND

FROM PRESENT
LIFETIME
BELIEF SYSTEMS

WHICH CREATES
CONFIRMING
BELIEF SYSTEMS

PRIMITIVE
MAN

YOU TEND TO
CREATE WHAT
YOU KNOW

RETURN PATH TO DISCOVERING
PRIMITIVE BELIEFS AND MEMORIES
THRU HYPNOTHERAPY, TRANCE,
MEDITATION, HOLOTROPIC BREATHWORK,
ETC.

PRIMITIVE
BELIEF SYSTEMS
PAST LIVES

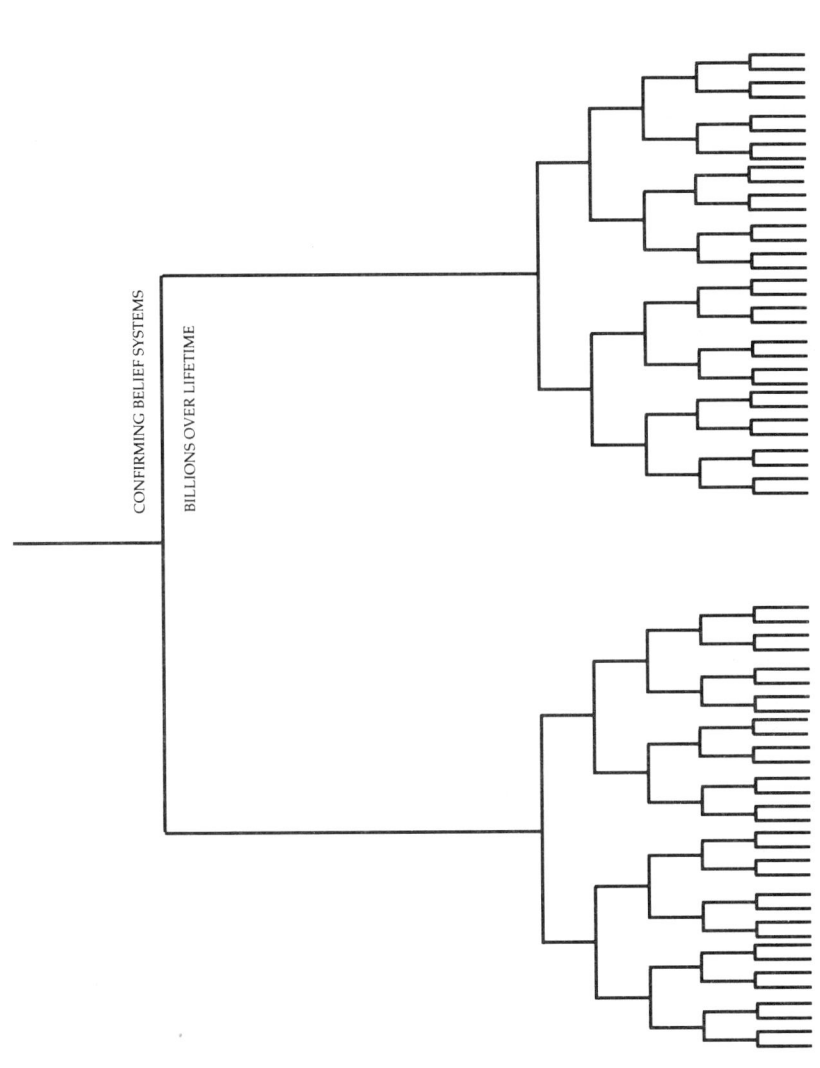

CONFIRMING BELIEF SYSTEMS

BILLIONS OVER LIFETIME

Chapter 18

DISCOVERING BELIEF SYSTEMS

It takes courage to discover and eliminate your belief systems. Other people can be guides, but only you know how you got to be the way you are. We can fool the world ,but not ourselves.

The ego is 100% belief systems. You are an exact and perfect representation of your present belief systems. Until these belief systems are discovered and eliminated, you cannot be anything else!

Upsets

To discover a belief system, all you need is an upset. Why?

If someone called you a yellow monkey, would you get upset? No, because you are not a yellow monkey! Therefore, if you are getting upset, it is not the person or the event that is upsetting you but the internal belief system.

The present upset is caused by the last upset or the initial upset. In any case, they will produce the same physical and emotional reaction every time.

So have an upset and <u>consciously</u> observe your feelings and emotions. What past memory image comes up? Try to get the earliest one. The initial controlling belief systems are few in number but very powerful.

Belief systems were formed when you were a child and

everything was out of proportion. You were tiny and powerless. Adults were big, powerful, controlled love, food, knowledge, fun, pain, activities, and time schedules, etc. You created belief systems to survive.

If I am <u>now</u> miserable, then at one time in my life I was miserable and survived. I am a 100% perfect reflection of my inside belief systems. Therefore, I have belief systems that say that to survive, I must be miserable." Believe me, it's very easy to discover your belief systems if you will start to play detective and observe your behavior.

The ego creates belief systems to survive. If, as a child, I break a bone and survive, then the ego sees the event as an act of survival. The belief system <u>could be</u> "In order to survive, I have to break a bone." In this case a person would look at his past life and have many broken bones; and never realize they were not accidents, but the result of a belief system.

If you fail a test and survive, you will fail a lot of tests and feel you're not as smart as other people; If you are rejected but survive, then you could form a belief system that the way to survive is to get rejected. To go a little further. If you almost die but survive, your life will have more than one near death experience because the way to survive is to almost die.

Therefore, your past life would be a series of events where you failed a lot of tests, experienced many rejections and near death experiences.

If you completely observe a lifetime habit like smoking, drinking, or over eating for one day you'll quickly see how belief systems trigger automatic behavior.

Every time you smoke, worry, feel guilty, bored, anxious, over indulge in food or drink, or get depressed about money, you have been triggered by a belief system.

So, it's not a problem to discover belief systems, the problem is that in most formations of belief systems we cannot remember the initial one. So we have to use whatever memory comes up and work backward.

Keep a Journal

Here is a list of questions to help you discover belief systems

What is your #1 upset?

Describe it in full detail. Write down everything you can remember about the event. The time of day, weather, emotions, feelings, age, smells, sounds, songs and sight.

What past memory is triggered when you see something, hear a song, smell, taste, or touch? For instance, you may eat or smoke when you feel uneasy, guilty, bored, or upset. What do you react to? When do you hesitate? Notice when your mood changes. What preceded it?

You will discover a belief system. Every memory is connected to a belief system. Soon a pattern will develop. Even if you only get part, you will feel better. A few hours will pass and more memories will come up.

Notice where your behavior is always the same. Do you always reward yourself the same way? Do you always celebrate a certain way? Do you do the same thing to celebrate as to reward yourself? Are they connected? Is there a pattern?

Give examples of it by recalling situations when it has come up. How many memories of situations of this incident do you have? How has it affected your life?

Remember, belief system combinations are endless. Relief of one will lead to relief of many. All of our senses are related not only to themselves, but to everything else in the body.

More Questions

Are you afraid?
Do you like the status quo?
What makes you insecure?
Do you laugh or smile when you are sad?
What situations do you avoid?
Are you happy, productive, truthful, and content about
  yourself?
When do you give up?
What do you like about yourself?
What do you dislike about yourself?
Do you assume something is going to happen for no reason
  and then get upset when it doesn't?
Are you always the first one to be convinced there is no
  solution to the problem?
When do you eat chocolate, ice cream, smoke a cigarette,
  twitch or bite your nails, scratch yourself, get constipated?
When do you get anxious, fearful, doubtful, fatigued, guilty,
  upset, angry, resentful, sexy, lustful, frustrated, sad, worry,
  sick to your stomach,etc,. Describe how it has done this.
Recall what your parents, teachers, friends, and accepted
  leaders have told you you ought to be;

What pressures to conform do you feel?
  a.   Peer
  b.   Family
  c.   Group
  d.   Religious

What is your first memory of it?

What punishment is administered for failure to comply?
  a.   Are you treated as an outcast?
  b.   Who made the rule?

     c.   Why was the rule made?

     d.   Who benefits from the rule?

     e.   Who loses from the rule?

     f.   Who justifies the rule?

What belief systems have you created as a result?

How is the belief system just discovered controlling you? How are the conditions then and now different? Was the belief system true then and now? Is it useful to you any more?

If an earlier belief system memory comes up, repeat process using the discovered belief system as the incident. What past event flashes in your mind? It may only flash for a 1/10 of a second. You will say, that's not it, but that's it! Write it down. Somehow, it connected to your belief system. You will sigh and take a tremendous deep breath when you hit bottom.

Soon you will identify similar actions repeating themselves. Then you will identify groups of actions repeating themselves.

What do you do with a past memory of a belief system you have discovered? Were you born with this belief system? If not, it's a belief system. Put it in your notebook and date it. Live with it.

Keep a similar journal for your children.

1.   Observe what belief systems the child has already inserted.

2.   By conversation and observation discover what belief systems people have that will come in contact with your children. Try to involve them in a group.

If the above seems all too impossible, it is not. Your consciousness is desperate to be free and will do all the work for you if you decide just to begin. Once you discover a belief system and experience eliminating it, you will never want to stop.

Discovering a belief system and eliminating it releases trapped energy. This inner wealth is in all of us waiting for the cork to pop and set us on a conscious new path.

Discovering a belief system will make you experience regret at all your past automatic unconscious behavior. That's the real price of losing a belief system. The reward is the future pleasure of the rest of your life without that belief system.

A dream is a very powerful opportunity to discover belief systems. Write the dream down in as much detail as possible. All the people in the dream are your creation. Therefore, you are each person in your dream. Investigate the belief system you are operating out of in each character in your dream.

Do you have Belief Systems in these areas?

social	you must have faith
group	trust God
religious	you can never know
family	mother knows best
marriage	girls - boys
divorce	do what you are told
boredom	do what I can
eating	forgiving
fear of being hurt:	respect
fear of abandonment	polite?
fear of Betrayal	commitment
fear of being naked	integrity
defeat by Superior:	
defeat by inferior	dignity
losing a loved one:	being considerate
resentment at feeling owned,	being tolerant
manipulated, used, etc.	compassion

resentment of needing to be
owned, used, etc.
resentment of needing to be
possessed
resentment of needing to be
suffocated
needing warmth - love, quiet
fear of losing trust - Self
esteem, power, sex.

breaking your word
self-exile
failure
theft
punishment
being neat
self-respect
being responsible
be a good boy - girl
diapers
toilet training
wetting bed
crawling
hugs
car trips
moving
anger
worry
anxiety
love
losing love

being just to all
being appreciated
being admired
shame
being sorry
harmful acts
gossip
goals
trust worthy
risk
lies
stupid
intelligence
average
working hard
being efficient - competent
superstition
compliments
heroes
demands
psychic
fortune tellers
children - babies
toys
games
grief
lazy
decency - indecency
insanity
possessions
your potential

cruelty
being ill
being dirty
weary - tired
hungry
sore teeth
dentist
unfaithful
faithful
alcohol - too much
accidents
arguments
drugs
jealously
vengeance
being a good example
looking good
order by areas - work - play
protecting; forest-plants, trees,
pollution
litter
evil
good will
personal property
traitor
propaganda
breaking laws
taxes
government
criminals
truth

obligation
rules
authority
conduct
being rich
being poor
being successful
ridicule
being a winner
being a loser
chaos
culture
lying
loyalty
betrayal
being tricked
self-control
honesty
rejection
grief
computers
modern appliances
arrogance
study
memorize
being wrong
being right
doing what is right
rehearsal - practice
tolerance race-creed-color
religion- yours - everyone else's
parents

Chapter 19

PREPARATIONS FOR DOING PROCESSES

Your ego is a survival machine and will violently resist eliminating belief systems! Its first defense is a covering belief system that says: "You do not have belief systems; it's silly to look for them; if people find out what you're trying to do, they'll think you're stupid."

Locating and eliminating this belief system is an essential part of beginning the journey to consciousness.

Documenting Your Progress

When you eliminate a belief system, document it! Unless you can refer back to your successes, your ego will say: "it's not working - stop doing it." And when you are down, you will listen and stop.

Make the longest list possible of belief systems to be removed. This list will be your record.

The Ever Present Collective Ego

Your ego and the collective ego is threatened by the elimination of belief systems and is dedicated 24 hours a day to get you to stop! How many times has your mind told you to stop reading this book?

Writing this book has been very difficult. If I succeed, my book will assist others to eliminate belief systems which threatens the powerful collective ego.

The result is that I write a few paragraphs and feel sleepy, lonely, confused, doubtful, insecure and cannot concentrate. I am stimulated to go to the bathroom, eat ice cream, and turn on the TV. Feelings of helplessness, hopelessness, and powerlessness overwhelm me. My ego helps me to remember all my past failures.

Each time you read this book, you too will feel sleepy, confused, hungry, discontented, or ill. A headache will come from nowhere. As you reread the book, you will be amazed at what you did not notice the first time. (Your ego made you unconscious!)

I suggest you use different color markers each time you read the book to verify what I have stated.

As you eliminate belief systems, more concentration will consciously surface to help you.

OTHER EGO OBSTACLES

A Clean Start

When a person decides to begin, the ego's first action is to activate an inserted belief system that we need a clean start. Example: You decide to go on a diet but don't start it.

There is no clean start in real life!

Every generation created and passed on belief systems and its just one big mess.

Removing belief systems is more like a dirty kitchen after a huge meal than a clean piece of paper. The only way to get a clean kitchen is to begin to clean it. A delay will not help. You have to dig your way out from where you are.

So start where you are (Your last upset) and handle whatever comes up.

Resistance to Change

The choice not to change is not a choice at all , but a unconsciousness belief system inserted by observation at a very young age. How? Lets imagine a room with fifty people who feel change is risky. Two people decide to make a change. One makes a change and good things happen. (49 people suffer envy.) The second person makes a change and bad things happen. (49 people shout to the world that change is bad.)

A child growing up would observe all of this and insert a belief system that change is bad. You go with the majority (another belief system).

Mind is Like a Computer

Our mind is very much like a computer, capable of enormous memory. To eliminate any part of the memory, you first have to bring it on the screen. Then, touch the elimination button.

Being conscious of a belief system memory is the same as being on the screen. Then, eliminate it by reliving it. Not on the screen equals not being conscious or automatic unconscious belief system behavior..

Using the Power of the Fear of Death to Unlock Belief Systems

Belief systems derive their power to control you from the fear of death. If you do not fear death, belief systems lose their power.

Core belief systems are formed with your whole body and mind at the fear of death level. If you were about to die, what body sensations would you experience? Primitive man was always vulnerable and in maximum danger of death and if he survived, intense emotions and feelings created a belief system which was very valuable to him because its use allowed him to survive.

Near Death Intensity

Learning how to use near death intensity is the key to discovering and eliminating belief systems. When you are doing a process, BE and feel the helplessness of primitive man in extreme danger doomed to die with no hope of rescue. That is the intensity level of the original belief system. This will create the energy to penetrate your covering belief systems and get to the original belief system.

When the human being recreates the experience consciously and experiences it with the same original emotional and physical conditions, it will disappear.

You are after the core belief system. Similar belief systems group together, with the most recent on the top and early-life ones on the bottom. When you eliminate a core belief system, all the confirming belief systems are eliminated. If you get the middle, all above the middle disappears. Sometimes you have to experience each one and other times you can get directly to the original.

You have to relive everything to be fully conscious. Even when you do these processes wrong you will relive and re-experience something. You can't lose. Since it all has to go, keep going.

You can always tell you are operating out of a belief system by asking, "Could I make myself anymore upset if I was about to die?"

Here is a simple test to verify the above statement.

Statement: "I am afraid I won't find the perfect mate."

Question:	What will happen if you don't find the perfect mate?
Answer:	I'll be lonely.
Question:	What will happen if you are forever lonely?
Answer:	I'll be miserable.
Question:	What will happen if you are forever miserable?
Answer:	I will get sick.
Question:	What will happen if you are forever sick?
Answer:	I will die!
Conclusion:	If you don't find the perfect mate, you are going to die.

Breaking a Hundred Dollar Bill

Collapsing a $100 bill or a core belief system is the same. If you find a need for a $10 or $20 and spend it, you will force the $100 bill to collapse into lesser amounts. If you locate a little belief system and eliminate it, you will collapse the major belief system.

There are many $100 bills in your life.

Let's examine guilt. I can have guilt belief systems about anything. I can be guilty about sex, having vague feelings that I'm evil, not doing anything meaningful with my life, or being overweight.

These guilt belief systems are not $100 bills, they are $10's and $20's! The $100 bill is that you have a belief system that says, "you should be guilty!" That in order to survive you have to be guilty! This is the controlling belief system and all the guilt belief systems cling to it. Take away the trunk and the branches will disappear. (See Misery Tree, Page 74)

The world will be a better place when there are less $100 bills in it. Do your part and get rid of yours, then your family and friends, your town, your state, your country, your universe.

Where will the energy come from? The answer will come to you when you remove your first belief system. You will feel so free, so delightful, so full of energy, there will be no question; only the answer.

All Memory is a Lie

Every childhood memory you have is a lie and is held in place as well as justified, by a belief system.

Unfortunately, our most powerful belief systems are formed when we are children and our perception and interpretation cannot help but be distorted.

Not the event, but the interpretation of the event forms the belief system. The person forming the belief system creates all the feelings and emotions of the characters in the event through their personal filter, the way it affected them, not the way the total event happened.

As one assumes the feelings and emotions of other people, the memory emerges as a lie. Since the memory justifies the belief system, the belief system is a lie too. Therefore, your belief system is predicated on a lie.

As children, we cannot know or perceive that a spanking, to stop us from crossing the street, was an act of love on our parents' part. We might perceive it as terror and pain and very threatening to our survival. The child's created belief system would have little relationship to the truth of the event.

Sometimes a child will inadvertently trigger a core belief system of a parent, which triggers primitive man within the parent and the reaction is so violent no child could correctly interpret it.

The resulting belief system created is also heavily charged with fear of violence. Anything that reminds the child of this belief system will create the fear of the violence in the original incident. Ultimately, any fear, however slight, will trigger total fear.

Misunderstandings also contribute towards the formation of belief systems. A child can misunderstand a single incident in childhood, and have it effect his or her life forever. A child remembers not only how they felt, but create the feelings and emotions of the other people involved in the event.

Any incident you survive can create a belief system. Your present memory of past belief systems is part of your everyday operating system and provides the boundaries of your life.

Your memories, those incidences you decided to remember, created what you consider to be your past life. Your past life was much more than your memories. What you consider your past life is your belief systems.

Eliminate your belief systems and your past will vanish. Who you are will change!

Thus, your memory is the road map to your belief systems. What memories do you have, and what belief systems have you created from them? Recalling any part of the memory, physical, emotional, smell, or touch could make you conscious of the total memory.

Experts tell us we store 100% of what we experience, but are only able to recall about three percent. Why do we remember only 3% of the many millions of incidents that occurred. These memories are hooks to justify your behavior and create your past.

One of my favorite stories about my father is that he kicked me for saving a high school friend from drowning. The truth is: My father did kick me and I did save a friend from drowning.

My father was a hard working man who loved and was very

proud of his son. The son was a rebel, a clown, and had no regard for authority. Father was constantly being notified by the police, the fire department, or the high school principal, of his son's unacceptable activities.

My father was filled with frustration and helplessness on this particular day because he had just been notified by the principal that I had been playing hookey for the umpteenth time. When I encountered him, he only knew I had not been at school. He kicked me for playing hookey, but I chose to remember that he kicked me because I saved my friend from drowning (both happened the same day).

By remembering it this way, I always justify what a bad guy my father was and what an unreasonable childhood I experienced. Therefore, I reasoned, my bad marks and lack of success was not my fault.

How could I blame my father and justify my life if I remembered the true incident?

Another Example:

Let's imagine the following scene:

An average family surrounding--three children ages 5, 4, and 4 months and a loving mother. She is exhausted from trying to take care of a new child, her other children, plus doing the house work and cooking the meals.

As the scene opens, the mother is bathing and giving loving tender attention to her small child. Its been a long morning. She is already far behind schedule, rushing to catch up. As a result, she has been inadvertently ignoring the other two children. The mother loves all the children, dearly and equally. This would be obvious to anyone familiar with this family.

Out of the many perceived as well as real incidences of lack of attention and love that makes up a child's history, for some reason this particular day's lack of attention, and this particular bath, disturbs the five year old child and makes him feel unloved. As a result the child requests the mother give him the same loving and tender attention by also giving him a bath.

From the mother's viewpoint, which she assumes is obvious to any reasonable person including her five year old (notice that the mother is now creating and assuming the emotions and feelings of the children involved and another lie is born), this request is ridiculous and she flippantly denies the request. The child, already in a state of vulnerability, is devastated by the denial and experiences horrible aloneness.

Neither the mother nor the other child will ever recall this incident. However, the five year old, <u>for some unexplained reason</u>, will carry this particular incident unconsciously forever, and use it to shape and form a belief system that his mother does <u>not</u> love him that will justify <u>not</u> loving his mother. Neither the mother nor the five year old child will know why they don't get along. This belief system, if not removed, will last until death.

The five year old <u>for some reason</u> especially needed love at that moment. This flippant, unnoticed denial by the mother, stung the child like a thousand bees. The child's perception is black and white, with no grey. He was unable to record the entire incident the way it happened because of his youth and the hurt he experienced.

In reality, the mother loved the child very much, but the five year old child perceived the denial as total rejection. He chose to create a belief system that his mother did not love him. The child felt like he would have to go it alone! "I survived by being rejected, therefore, in order to survive, I must seek rejection."

The belief system from that moment on shields out all loving attention given after that by his mother. This blockage only confirms the rejection. Over a period of time, the ego accumulates thousands, millions of confirming rejections to justify the original belief system. This grown man may have a long history of women rejecting him.

The five year old operates his whole life out of this belief system automatically and unconsciously by recalling the original incident briefly and unconsciously when challenged in some way.

Assembling All People Involved

When an incident like this is discovered and all persons involved are interviewed, an entire different set of circumstances and perceptions emerge.

The event did happen, but the adult's memory of it and the child's interpretation of the event are different. Usually, the child was at least partially mistaken and unable to understand, integrate, and record the entire situation as it happened.

Assembling all the people involved has outstanding wonderful results; because it clears up for everyone why they have been treating each other so poorly. Much love follows.

Unfortunately, the ego never allows this. Most events just happens and we seldom notice it. We just obey the belief system.

Consider this example of a belief system causing great harm and emotional pain that was never personally observed:

Mr. Jones is 35 years old. He holds both a masters and Ph.D. He is very successful. He does not work on weekends. He is divorced. He has not lived at home since he was 17-years-old. Every Saturday morning he gets up at 7 a.m. and leaves the house, even though he hasn't anywhere to go, and returns about 4 p.m. When he was married, this used to drive his wife nuts. Until it was brought to his attention, he was unaware that he had done it every Saturday all his adult life.

Mr. Jones finally recalled that on Saturday, if he was still in the house as a boy when his father got up, he would get tasks assigned for the whole day. If he was not at home, it didn't happen.

The belief system was, "If you don't want to work all day Saturday, get out of the house early." He returned about 4 p.m. because of a similar reason. That was the time his father left for work.

His whole face lit up when he discovered this and he hardly ever left the house early on Saturdays after that. The most important change was that he started being aware and discovered other belief systems.

Do you have similar behavior? Do you wash the car every Sunday, even though it is raining?

Information and Advice on Discovering Belief Systems

Combination and confirming belief systems form around the core or original belief system. All anxiety belief systems will form around the original anxiety belief system (and over many lifetimes). Same with worry or grief.

Using lemons as an example:

The first lemon created a belief system about lemons. The second lemon created a combination of the first and second lemon belief systems and the third, etc. into the millions, each depending on the one before. Each lemon incident has either an identical or similar emotional and physical charge as the original.

By creating the emotional and physical charge of a recent

lemon incident, you can cause the mind to remember an early image or the original lemon incident Once you discover the core belief system, it will begin to dissolve and lose its power to control you in one of the following ways:

A.   You observe it and realize that the circumstances under which the belief system was created are no longer valid.

You were always afraid of the dark and remember when your Father locked you in a dark room to punish you when you were four years old. You realize <u>NOW</u> you are not four years old and whenever you face the dark in the future, you will remember the first incident; remember you are not four years old and not relive the original incident.

B.   You can relive the original incident by creating it from memory over and over feeling all the sensations and emotions until they lose their charge.

C.   Combinations of the above.

Whenever you consciously create a past memory, you will automatically reexperience the event and either zero-out the belief system or it will go away over time.

Sometimes you will not get the original belief system, but one that is blocking your mind from revealing the original. Experience the blocking belief system and look for another past memory. At first it will appear you have very few of these; but as you keep doing processes, you will constantly run into variations as you keep probing and going deeper into your mind or down to the trunk of the tree, so to speak.

Sometimes no past memory will occur. Some belief systems are so buried they do not flash long enough to be acknowledged. Others flash for 1/1000 of a second. That's it! Acknowledge it and do a process on it. Say everything you can remember about it.

Do belief system processes with others when it is particularly difficult. Your ego sets up defenses so you cannot see, but has no defenses against other people's observations.

A second person or a group can watch your face and body for reactions you personally might miss while doing the process. You might wince, stiffen, twitch or twiddle your fingers. They can notice and bring your attention to that moment in time. The more difficult the belief system is, the greater the release when you reexperience it.

Our task is to eliminate every unconscious belief system. When you consider the forced conditioning society inflicts upon us in the developmental era untouchable by memory, and that unconscious belief systems are not penetrated by facts, arguments, analysis or even a simple desire to change, the task seems beyond our scope. However, do not despair.

Consciousness has been struggling for 5 billion years to surface. Tremendous energy is created by eliminating a belief system. Imagine removing guilt or worry not only from your life, but from all your future generations. What a way to make a difference! How delightful!

The next chapter contains the Belief System Elimination Processes. My suggestion is to do them and let the researchers and scientists try to understand how they work.

When you experience an emotional memory physically and mentally it will be accompanied by a release of physiological tension, a feeling of extra energy, a deep breath and a calm, relaxed feeling. The memory will lose it ability to control you. Eliminating a controlling past event creates the possibility of a new future. Good Luck.

Chapter 20

BELIEF SYSTEM ELIMINATION PROCESSES (BSEP)

It's common psychiatric knowledge that if a person can be induced to reexperience (relive) a past event, it will lose its emotional charge. In other words, it will lose its ability to control you.

There are many methods and combinations of methods to eliminate belief systems.

Therapy

When you relate a past incident to a therapist, the degree that you consciously reexperienced the event physically and emotionally determines the extent the same event will trigger you in the future.

Nature's Way of Eliminating a Belief System

All of us have experienced losing a loved one. Unfortunately, your belief systems about your loved ones do not die with the loved one. They live inside you and bring sadness and tears unexpectedly.

A funeral is a good example of this when people suddenly remember a past incident and relieve it by either bursting into tears of sorrow or joy.

Birthdays and holidays are especially emotional as we remember loved ones. When we remember, we partially reexperience the original event and weaken the belief system.

The second year around there is less energy and emotion because the memories (belief system) have been relived once already.

This is nature's way of eliminating a belief system.   This process is automatic over a period of time (lifetimes and centuries) and automatically triggers itself. It could be done all at once by reexperiencing each memory over and over until it loses its energy.

The trick is to review your life to locate the experience that inserted the initial trigger and reexperience that event. When we remember a sad experience in our past and burst into tears, we are reexperiencing that event. If we continue reexperiencing the event, it will lose its power to trigger tears anymore.

Vague Controlling Belief System Elimination Process

How can you do a process when you can't identify feelings, emotions, and attitudes enough to relate them ? The answer is in the question! Who do you want to relate the information to? To your inner self. Your outer self wants to relate the information to your inner self. How convenient!

Your inner self knows precisely what is taking place within you, since it simultaneously experiences everything you think and feel. Therefore, just say: "We will merge consciously and experience what I cannot describe and eliminate it right now." If you persist and stay conscious, A deep breath will signal that you are achieving results.   A few moments will pass, but it will arrive.

If you stay conscious and do the above, scores of unconscious hard to define or explain moods can be eliminated with noticeable well being and increased awareness.

Mostly, you won't have a past memory or understand what has happened but you will feel better and the uncomfortable mood will not be there anymore. In a few weeks, you notice an increasing feeling of calmness about yourself and increased frequency of insights.

If there is a lot of energy on the belief system, a memory will surface. Otherwise, don't worry as long as you feel better You don't have to know the origin to eliminate it. When it's gone, who cares?

Some controlling belief systems are only triggered on certain dates. Anniversaries, birthdays, holidays, vacation, fireworks, or by the first snow or storms, etc.; a minor lifetime event at a single rare moment in time. You feel strange and in a weird mood. It's a vague controlling belief system.

Major Upset Belief System Elimination Process

Don't be afraid of doing a process. It's very easy when you overcome your fear of it which is a belief system. Fake the feeling and emotion. Fake it till you make it!

Describe your incident. Here are three examples to help you.

1.   Male: When I want to ask a girl to dance, I experience uncontrollable fear. My heart pounds, blood rushes to my head, my hands tremble, and my legs feel weak. It's difficult to breathe; and my chest feels like I have an iron band around it. I get tremendous feelings of anger and disgust at myself for being such a wimp.

2.   Female: When I go out on a date, I am unable to choose what to wear. I feel inadequate, insecure, afraid, unsure, nervous; and I cry. I have difficulty moving my legs, arms, and fingers. I'm always late and as a result, people consider me unorganized and a chowder head.

3.   When my mother is coming to visit, I suffer tremendous anxiety. I feel everything will go wrong and it will be my

fault.   My heart pounds.   I can hardly breathe; and I'm totally exhausted all the time.

What is the most upsetting thing in your life? Choose only one incident. Do not be vague. Write it down in your book as clearly as you can and everything about the event or incident you can recall. What is the name of your incident?

Choose a quiet place where you can relax and not be disturbed. Consciously, make a decision that what you are doing is valid, will succeed and give yourself permission to release all belief system information.   Close your eyes, calm down, relax, breathe deeply.

When a deep breath occurs, create the incident that is bothering you. Remember the last time it absolutely upset you. Not the last time it happened, but the last time it absolutely upset you.

Be with the incident as if you were there. Let yourself be totally upset physically and emotionally as you were at the time. (DOES A PAST MEMORY COME UP?) If not, break it down into parts as follows:

Emotional: ANXIETY -- can you recall the anxiety?
GUILT -- can you recall the guilt?   HATE?   RAGE? ANGER?   RESENTMENT?   FRUSTRATION?   DOUBT? FATIGUE?   FEAR?   FEAR OF LOSING LOVE, BEING ABANDONED, NOT GETTING APPROVAL, BEING EXPELLED, HUMILIATED, HATED, FORGOTTEN.   WHAT PAST MEMORY COMES UP? Go into as much detail as possible.

Physical: What physical sensations did you feel? Can you feel them now?--face flush, face tingle, mouth dry, gums hurt-tingle, stiff neck, eyes hurt, dry throat, head ache, head pressure. jaw rigid, teeth grinding each other, pain in chest-tightness, unable to breathe, stomach full of acid-burning, muscles tense-tight stiff, pain in knees, joints, toes, etc.? Go into as much detail as possible.

Does a past memory come up? TAKE A DEEP BREATH.

If not, what is your attitude about the incident? What would your attitude be if you saw someone else experiencing the incident instead of you? What would you say to that person? Where did this attitude come from? Does this bring up a past memory? BE COMPLETE!

If not, see yourself in the incident--How do you appear? Is your body rigid? Are you standing straight or slumped? Does this bring up a past memory? BE COMPLETE!

If not, review the incident for any material or information that has been left out. What has <u>not</u> been mentioned that is significant to this process? A smell or odor, a breeze, a color, a dream etc.? Empty your mind. What memory does this bring up?

Whenever you get a memory, however small or bizarre, however quickly it flashes, however irrelevant it may seem, it is important! It is a clue. Don't say that's not it. It flashed into consciousness for a reason. Don't let it slip away. Say whatever comes up into the recording machine.

Do not try to understand a belief system or how it was inserted in you. You do not pick up a belief system in any logical way. "Look before you leap," or, "To hesitate is to be lost" are contradictory, but we all operate out of both of them at different times. How or why it got there isn't important. Most belief systems will disappear when viewed consciously because they don't make any sense.

As you get familiar with the procedure, you can repeat it all day long. Good luck!

Here is an example of a process by the author: The belief system is, "I MUST BE MISERABLE TO SURVIVE."

How does it <u>feel</u> to be miserable?

Tense neck, blood rushing to my face, a feeling of pressure around the neck, congestion, stress, tightness in legs and arms.

What <u>emotions</u> are you experiencing?

Overpowering feeling that no matter what I attempt, the universe will find a way to make me fail. Even if I succeed, something else will come up. Happiness is unattainable, hopeless, helpless, forlorn, no solution, who cares, so what, what does it matter?

Attitude?

Give up, give in, don't try.

Body structure?

Caved in.

What memory or memories comes up?

As a child, I was told or led to believe or misunderstood that I had killed God. I didn't know how or when I did it, but never questioned it. We nailed him to the cross and let him die. How could I ever be forgiven for that? I was a goner.

Everything was helpless and hopeless as far as changing my life. I believed everybody I knew was a sinner, born with sin, full of guilt for what we had done to God. Only luck and God's mercy stood between me and everlasting hell. There was no escape.

My parents, teachers, all adults and everybody I knew was in the same boat. We all knew we were helpless.

Worry, anxiety, guilt, were never absent. Don't let anyone see you having a good time or smiling. They will think you are sinning. I was reminded about it every Sunday by seeing Christ on the cross and hearing lectures about sin. My parents and other adults believed all of it so it must be true.

My mother was miserable and worried about everything conceivable. Every future incident had 100 possible consequences that had to be worried about. My father was insecure and full of anxiety and anger. He was also miserable.

All I experienced my whole childhood was people being miserable, "AND I SURVIVED;" and the result was all of the above became belief systems.

Being aware (conscious) of all these made me realize that it wasn't true. That I was constantly reacting to the same events that happened years ago when I had no way to understand or integrate it.

The core belief system, the trunk of the tree began to dissolve. All the little guilts that nag me everyday fell away. I felt wonderful! It took weeks to completely leave me but it was one glorious breakthrough after another.

You may discover a very pleasant belief system. Great. Keep it but do it consciously from now on, not automatically. Know when you do it and why, own it consciously.

Each belief system that is discovered and eliminated will change the world.

The worst belief system is the one that says, "You are <u>not</u> God." The next worst is the one that states, "You can't know who you are and/or you can't know your belief systems."

Who would make a good partner for you to work with in eliminating belief systems?

_____

How about forming a group?

_____   _____

_____   _____

_____   _____

_____   _____

Chapter 21

CHANGING THE WORLD

Conversions

There are no quantum leaps in changing the world. Changing the world boils down to choosing to change the world. You cannot change another person's world. He must choose to change it!

When you remove a belief system, you will feel free, happy full of energy and want to share.

Unfortunately, the experience cannot be expressed and describing it to a friend will not get your friend's approval, cooperation, or agreement to join the journey of eliminating belief systems.

It sounds like gibberish to other people. You appear to be unreasonably happy, and you look and act like you feel terrific. This type of behavior seems strange and nutty to your friends.

Imagine walking up to your best friend who you have always loved because she shares the same guilty feelings you do and saying, "I have no feelings of guilt! They are gone!" Your best friend would take you to a doctor.

The right brain talking to another brain could do it, but the left mind is covered with belief systems that facts and actions cannot penetrate.

People will not believe what you say no matter how trustful

People will not believe what you say no matter how trustful and close the relationship is. In fact, it turns people off! Conversely, you cannot understand why others will not look at the opportunity to experience it.

People that live through a "near death" experience say very pleasant things regarding the moment. They, themselves never fear death again, but all the rest of us still do. When Saul became Paul on the road to Damascus only Saul was converted.

Before it happened to you, you would have acted the same way. They will not believe you until they experience it themselves. Conversion happens simultaneously with the elimination of a belief system.

Hear it Loud and Clear - Conversions Happen One at a Time!

People fear change. Many belief systems warn against change. Eliminating belief systems is a seemingly dangerous and risky enterprise.

If all the people in your life want the status quo, they will <u>not</u> change or encourage you to change. "So what, you'll get over it," or "bug off" is a normal response.

There is little choice here for you. You will not give up eliminating belief systems. The more belief systems you eliminate, the more separate and different you will appear to the group that continue to hold the old belief systems. The implication is that they are still right and you are a little weird.

Once you start to change, you will affect the people around you. In so far as you change, they will have to adjust. A stationary billiard ball does not create problems for the other balls on the table; but once it starts to move, all the other balls are going to get moved whether they like it or not.

be conscious of the effect it will have on the people you consider important in your life. The solution is to go slow. If they don't approve, let it be.

Wait for the right opportunity when they are upset and sit them down, ask the right questions about feelings and emotions, etc.; and see if they can remember a past incident. If they do remember and take a deep breath, you can explain how the past incident is controlling them.

When it works, it won't matter if they understand. However, this will better explain why you are different now. You will have converted a friend to take the journey with you.

Permission

Most people have a belief system that says they need approval before they change and that includes you!

Where change is encouraged by the group, change will happen. The group supports them against the outside status quo pressures.

For example, AA has meetings where members mutually support each other, give strength, love, and encouragement to change. Revival meetings are similar. People will do what gets them love and approval.

How to Begin

Someone has to begin. Declare your intention and people will polarize around you. They will support you in forming the group, and that support will give you the power you need to lead it. Search and discover people who are into eliminating belief systems. The most energy will come from this self-created environment.

Get your family to read the book and realize how many belief systems you have in common. Then your relatives, friends, the town, the city, the country, the world.

Many belief systems are passed down from generation to generation. Can you imagine removing stress, guilt and worry forever in all future generations of your family? What a gift to your offspring!

Every belief system discovered and removed makes the world now and forever a better place to be. If your children are not given belief systems, can you imagine the consciousness they will have to create a better world, and the cumulative effect over time.

The journey of a thousand miles begins with the first step and that step is you. Discover and eliminate a belief system and help someone else do the same. If everyone who reads this book does that, no power on earth will prevent the return journey of human beings to consciousness.

In the final analysis, what works will survive regardless of the opposition. The people at the bottom discover that the method works and start using it and slowly, society accepts it. So, if you want to change the world, go to the bottom, not to the top!

The information in this book has helped me tremendously and if it works for you, enjoy it regardless of what people say. You can change the world by changing yourself.

Chapter 22

THE UNIVERSE DOESN'T CARE

How disgusted God must be with us. He creates a paradise and a few billion years later, he returns to find a bunch of loonies full of pain, disease, resentment, worry, pride, anxiety, glory, greed, with few inhabitants enjoying the place.

Get Conscious!

You are going to die! Time cannot be saved and stored like money and gold. The earth and all its people have survived without Jesus, Buddha, Popes, and Kings, and they will make it without you.

Become conscious of this. Everybody gets so much time and when it's gone, you're gone. Draw a line from one to 80 years and put yourself on it. Not much time left is there?

When you die, you will not be asked what you did with your money, or what people were impressed by you. You are going to be asked, "Did you enjoy God's paradise?"

Did you do what you really wanted to do? What are you waiting for?

This Moment Is It!

People are always waiting for wonderful things to happen to them. You are wonderful right now and belief systems prevent you from being conscious of it. Waiting for IT to happen is a waste of time! If there is an IT, this very moment is IT! Heaven is "right here now" on earth hidden from you by belief systems! There is nothing else ahead or behind you, but more moments.

"On the Way to Heaven is Heaven"

There is only the path. Whatever moment you are in right now is your position on the path. What you experience on the path, moment to moment is what you are here to learn. There is no meaning to your life except to enjoy the moment. So enjoy the pain, the sorrow, the grief, and the love and keep doing processes. It's your life and your moments.

If we pollute the earth, drop a thousand atomic bombs and every human being disappears from the earth, it will go on. It has for 15 billion years and it will continue.

Be Divine
Be a Heroic Vitalist!

The message of the universe is, if you want divine power and energy, follow your heart, do what delights and interests you. You can't take your money with you, but you can enjoy everyday by doing work that gives you a feeling of accomplishment.

Do what you want to do for no reason. Get a magnifying glass and look at a flower, a rock or a grain of sand. Enjoy the flow, feel the energy of the universe.

Go for it with all your heart and enjoy every moment of it. Work and play consciously and enjoy. Live in such a way that yesterday was great, today is better, and tomorrow, better still.

When you make this shift, quality of life becomes more important than material accumulation. You enjoy everything, eating, conversation, sex, music, work, and nature.

Your belief systems lose their power once you realize this life will end.

When you die, your loved ones and friends will adjust. There might be some weeping and wailing from the family but if you leave a little money and property, they will recover rapidly. The rest of your close friends will forget you as soon as next month's bills arrive. They have no choice. Life is about survival, not death.

Let other people be, and don't worry what they think or say. They are doing the best they can with their present belief systems. If they're watching you instead of going for it themselves, feel sorry for them.

Besides, since you are going to die, what difference does it make?

Chapter 23

CONSCIOUSNESS

Our birth right and on heritage is consciousness.

When we talk about consciousness, it may sound very difficult. Let me tell you that nobody understands it, so don't worry. To be fully conscious is to be God and God not being of time or space cannot be understood by time and space beings, who have belief systems.

Just begin by discovering a belief system of your own and removing it. Taking out belief systems will increase your consciousness. The more consciousness you attain, the more wonderful your life will be.

This whole book is really about consciousness.

Lots of people more intelligent than I am have written about consciousness on a very high level. The intention of <u>1st Grade Therapy for Adults</u> is to get you started so you will seek out these authors for further information.

In the meantime, here is a summary of statements about consciousness:

Consciousness is what we all have in common. Before belief systems, we were consciousness. A cup of liquid, a swimming pool, a river, an ocean, coffee, tea, milk, sludge, urine, steam, plants, and vegetables are separate and different but they have water in common.

Consciousness:

> equals God.
> knows all is also one.
> must <u>be</u>, it cannot, <u>Not be</u>.
> cannot be held--it creates itself and becomes a thought and vanishes.
> is the ability to create.
> is where spirit and matter meet.
> is not partial. Like the sun, it will shine on all things.
> is beyond space and time.
> is still within us, and includes time and space.
> belongs to spirit. It is not part of the body.
> is loving and not being afraid.
> is love and tolerance sharing and serving others because they are we.
> is what many people call the soul or spirit.
> is the act of staying in the present through every emotion.
> is simultaneous action and acknowledgment.
> allows people to act for the good of all.
> allows us to love other people.
> equals a perfect body.
> hampered by belief systems equals a sick body.
> is the physical material of the spirit formed into flesh.
> is not being controlled by belief systems.
> forgetting itself becomes a belief system.
> is engaged elsewhere if you have a blank stare.

Conscious and unconscious are one and the same separated by belief systems.

Consciousness does not lie in the future, but inside us in the present, trapped and dominated by major, controlling, and primitive belief systems. We do not have to create it. We have to reveal it to ourselves by eliminating belief systems.

Every change for the better has been created by a burst of

consciousness. When you day dream or meditate, it slips through the belief system cracks. You call it intuition or insight.

Once you have a thought it doesn't vanish. A new idea has a consciousness. When friends get together and exchange ideas and create new ones, they are creating new consciousness for each other. It can be recalled forever. It does not disappear like a belief system experienced.

However, you don't have a belief system about how it happens or how to make it happen more often, or how to make it happen when you want it to happen. You cannot validate it, even though it's the most valid thing in your life.

When you are experiencing consciousness, you are not conscious of it. There is no one seeing and nothing being seen. Seeing and seen merge. It is a special timeless moment when we are one with the universe. We know it by our memory of it.

An orgasm is a good example. It was a merge, a timeless moment when spirit and matter, consciousness and unconsciousness all merged. Your experience of it is a memory. When you recall it, you will recall the memory of the experience, not the experience. However, the experience was consciousness. The memory is a belief system. We as ego were not there.

Consciousness is the actual merging experience of the pleasure. Memory or belief system is the, "was" of the pleasure. Memory or belief system is the past, not the actual pleasure. Consciousness is always new, always a merge. Not repeatable. We chase the memory of the experience of consciousness. The belief system is all that remains.

A merge (consciousness = now) can seem like an eternity and yet there is no feeling of time or space. Do you remember the initial blushing of young love, the first time you saw your first born?

When you play a sport and keep your attention on the ball, you are conscious. When you miss or mess up, then your ego = belief system takes over and tells you what went wrong or shows up as anger or stated as, "Oh, shit! I missed."

When you were one with the ball, you were experiencing consciousness. Your memory of it is a belief system. You can have a desire to return to the consciousness you have experienced, but that is a belief system. You cannot return.

Consciousness has no pleasure or sorrow. Consciousness is. It is, 100%! There is no room for what else. What else is a belief system. As you read this paragraph, you are one with the paragraph. You are a merge with the paragraph.

I knocked you out of the merge by interrupting your attention. Where were you before I interrupted you? You came after you remembered it. During the merge, you were not there, only consciousness was there.

A Deep Breath

When a belief system is formed, it forms in all parts of the body. If the belief system was formed during a period of tenseness or stress, the muscles will be rigid all the time and the body will get used to that; and you will not notice it.

When consciousness arrives, belief systems are disengaged, the body relaxes and a deep breath is possible. Almost all deep breaths are the results of flashes of consciousness.

Consciousness comes when the mind is in neutral. You will take a deep breath just after it arrives. Just after it's been there.

In consciousness, belief systems are acknowledged and disappear.

You are conscious when a belief system is formed. That is, you are conscious <u>at</u> the event or the forming of the belief system. From then on, the belief system makes you unconscious. Conversely, when a belief system is acknowledged and eliminated, you are also conscious. When you operate automatically from the belief system, you are <u>not</u> conscious.

Belief systems are within time and space. A belief system can be, then <u>be</u> reexperienced and eliminated and then <u>not be</u>.

Our ego is the sum total of our belief systems and belief systems do not exist in a state of consciousness. We are separated by our belief systems. Belief systems cause us to go from consciousness to automatic behavior.

Separation is the opposite of consciousness. Our belief systems about our bodies, religions, nationalities, money, intelligence, manners, rituals, prevent us from realizing we are one consciousness. All human beings, regardless of race, creed, or color, are so similar that it takes tremendous belief systems to prevent us from realizing or seeing it. We are all one consciousness.

You are conscious. The rest is a shell of belief systems. What happens to the shell is what most people spend their whole life trying to figure out. Yet, it is not important. The conscious person can make clean judgements about their position in reality. People with belief systems cannot.

Look into another person's eyes and you cannot escape the knowledge you are one with that person. "I have seen this person before." "I know this person." "You and I are one feeling." Have you known this person in the past or is he or she you in the present?

If all of the present belief systems are removed, we are only left with our consciousness with everything, everywhere and nowhere. Since I am you and you are I, how can I not be for you? Our very experience of life would evolve into the golden rule.

Consciousness, Many Kinds

Consciousness is what enables us to know people through other means than just our five senses. They allow us to merge into other creatures and know their lives.

Why do we feel so good when walking in the woods or by the ocean, playing with a dog, breathing fresh air, taking a sunbath, looking at the stars, etc.? Merging with a great consciousness increases our vitality.

We have, as a society, few belief systems about nature, compared with religion, sex, food, sweets, tobacco, anxiety, guilt, worry, stress, etc. (It never occurred to power seeking people to control nature. How do you control a cyclone?) Therefore, it's easy to merge consciousness with nature.

A tree to a human has a certain consciousness. We experience it as a tree. How would a bird, an ant, a wood worm, a squirrel, experience a tree? When a human's consciousness merges with a tree's consciousness, is this merged consciousness the same as when a squirrel's consciousness merges with the tree's consciousness?

How about the merge of a bird and a squirrel? an ant and a bird? a squirrel and a cat?

Consciousness is being one with all animals, including insects. Look into their eyes. Rocks, plants, vegetables, animals are consciousness.

We are with them because of consciousness, but belief systems prevent us from knowing it. Possibly, we have more potential for consciousness than other earth objects, but most humans use it the least.

The precision of music is consciousness common to all people. When you experience hearing music, the joy comes from the merging of your consciousness with the consciousness of the music, and all who ever heard the music. Hearing music written centuries ago is a merging of consciousness over time and space.

Different conscious realities must be beyond numbers.

Single Consciousness

In Africa, there is a coral colored flower that is not a flower.

Flattid bugs are found in Africa. When the bugs land, they form what appears to be a coral colored flower. The purpose is to create protection from its enemies (birds) who are looking for bugs, not flowers. Each blossom of the flower is a wing of an insect. The flower is green at the top, partially colored next, and then a pure coral. Each batch of eggs includes one bug with green wings, several with in-between shades, the rest, pure coral.

If you shake the branch, the bugs will disperse. When they land again, they will assemble themselves instantly in the correct arrangement of the flower. <u>And, the flower the bugs are imitating does not exist in nature!</u>

Can anyone doubt these bugs have a consciousness in common? They are separated, single, and individual, but become one because of a collective need. Do humans have this gift still to be discovered?

Another example of common consciousness is schools of fish. Observing them will reveal instant turns of direction. There is no leader, the group is a single consciousness.

Consciousness, Paradise, Heaven

Consciousness in it's total essence is similar to encountering the being of light and love often described by people who have had near death experiences. People say the experience cannot be expressed in words.

Heaven is a paradise defying description and we cannot see it, use it, appreciate it.

Paradise is described as a garden of incredible beauty full of blossoming trees and tame animals, rivers and lakes that have clear water that sparkles.

Paradise is further described as a metaphysical ecstasy separated from the rest of us by an insurmountable something. Each religion has its own barriers or belief systems.

1. High mountain
2. Large island
3. Region at end of earth
4. Impassable wall
5. Barrier of ice
6. Dense perpetual fog
7. Curtain of fire

Death takes us through the barrier to paradise. Paradise is earth, in the present with no pollution, or belief systems. Without belief systems we would not need death to get us where we already are.

Consciousness is paradise on earth without belief systems.

We conceived it, therefore, we can attain it right now. We created the barriers separating us from paradise. The barriers are belief systems. Remove them and you will have consciousness or paradise.

A fully conscious person would be one with the universe. We are on a long journey to reach this goal. However, as the Chinese say, "A journey of a thousand miles begins with the first step."

The elite have passed the 500 mile mark and the rest of us have yet to take the first step. Once you learn how to remove a belief system, you will zoom forward.

We are a piece of God. God, the past, present, and future are hidden by belief systems of all sorts, including space and time.

A Way of Being Instantly Consciousness

A belief system cannot operate in the present. If you can stay conscious, belief systems cannot control you.

Concentrate on your breathing. Total attention on your breathing transports you to the "now" or present moment. Follow your breath in and out of your body. Breathe into any part of your body, into any anxiety, pain or nervousness and it will go away. Closing your eyes will enhance your ability to do this exercise.

The ego tries to make you feel you and it are identical. And when you lose a belief system, it is a partial death. What is being diminished is not you, but your ego and what is being increased is your consciousness.

The Future

Every limitation we perceive is a belief system. Who we are right now and who we will be in the future is controlled by our belief systems. By eliminating your belief systems you will change who you are and what you can be in the future. It is all in your power.

Within 50 years, our level of consciousness will rise until we can see and communicate with other beings not solid in nature.

Psychics are doing it right now. It will become as common as the telephone.

We will imagine or desire it and it will be. We will see the future that we are presently creating and be able to change it by imagining it the way we want it to be. We will merge time and space so we can see past, present, and future. We will see and discover how to communicate with other forces of existence, including plants and animals.

This communication will lead to an understanding so deep and vast that none of us will be able to imagine doing what is not right for all. We will understand how our actions affect ourselves and our other existences. Wars and pollution will stop. We will share our resources. Hunger will cease.

DO NOT PUT THIS BOOK ON THE SHELF.

KEEP IT MOVING.

LOAN IT TO A FRIEND OR RELATIVE

Name	Date Loaned	Date Returned
1._____	_____	_____
2._____	_____	_____
3._____	_____	_____
4._____	_____	_____
5._____	_____	_____
6._____	_____	_____
7._____	_____	_____
8._____	_____	_____
9._____	_____	_____
10._____	_____	_____

ORDER FORM

Wayne Smith Company
1300 L Street, N.W.
Suite 1050, Box A
Washington, D.C. 20005
(202)484-5620

"1st Grade Therapy for Adults"

by Jack Bogasky

$11.95 U.S

Yes, I would like to order _____ copies of
1st Grade Therapy for Adults.

> Shipping charges:
> First book: $2.00
> Additional books $1.00 each

Books	$_____
Book rate shipping	$2.00
Handling Charge	$0.75
TOTAL	$_____

DC Residents subject to a 6% Sales tax.

☐ Check Enclosed ☐ Mastercard
☐ American Express ☐ Visa

Name on Card _____

Card # _____

Expiration Date _____

Signature _____

To order by phone, please call (202)484-5620
Or fax your order to (202)898-0484.

Name _____

Organization _____

Address _____

City, State, Zip _____

Telephone _____